CONTENTS

Feminist Review is published three times a year by a collective based in London, with help from women and groups all over the UK.

The Collective: Alison Light, Alison Read, Annie Whitehead, Catherine Hall, Clara Connolly, Dot Griffiths, Erica Carter, Helen Crowley, Loretta Loach, Lynne Segal, Mary McIntosh, Mica Nava, Naila Kabeer, Sue O'Sullivan.

Correspondence and advertising
For contributions and all other correspondence please write to:
Feminist Review, 11 Carleton Gardens, Brecknock Road, London N19 5AQ.
For advertising please write to:
David Polley, Routledge, 11 New Fetter Lane, London EC4P 4EE

Subscriptions
Please write to: Subscriptions Department, Routledge Journals, Cheriton House, North Way, Andover, Hants SP10 5BE.

Contributions
Feminist Review is happy to discuss proposed work with intending authors at an early stage. We need copy to come to us in our house style with references complete and in the right form. We can supply you with a style sheet. Please send in 4 copies plus the original (5 copies in all). In cases of hardship 2 copies will do.

Bookshop distribution in the USA
Routledge, Chapman and Hall, Inc. 29 West 35th Street, New York, NY10001, USA.

Typeset by Type Study, Scarborough
Printed in Great Britain
at the University Press, Cambridge

ISSN 0141-7789

Cover illustration: 'Another Way of Seeing Diana' from *The Cancer Drawings of Catherine Arthur*.

We would like to apologize to Clara Connolly for publishing in *Feminist Review* 39, the letter on her article 'Splintered Sisterhood: Antiracism in a Young Women's Project'. Although we like to keep the letters page as open as possible, it is not our policy to publish letters which contain personal criticism. On reflection we felt that publication of this letter was a mistake.

Feminist Review Collective

EDITORIAL

In this issue we have several articles dealing with the theme of women and health. The major one addresses the medicalizing and marketing of the menopause and osteoporosis, based on the experience from the USA. In Britain the National Health Service still exists, though seriously underfunded and threatened by creeping privatization, and that has important effects on our health care. What market forces tap into and create in the USA, however, heralds the direction changes will take here, changes which are already well under way in the case of the promotion of treatments for the menopause. This article reminds us that the issue of women's health, and our control over our own bodies, however tenuous, is not bounded by reproduction. In the early years of Women's Liberation, critiques of the medical establishment concentrated on reproductive health. Today all the more general issues of health and illness throughout a lifetime, including living our dying, have become central issues for feminists.

In this issue, as well as putting together a patchwork of AIDS pieces which give a taste of the various ideas and projects happening in different countries around women and HIV, and the consistent failure of so much of professional AIDS education to address the needs and interests of women as sexual agents, we reproduce some of the cancer drawings of Catherine Arthur, which illustrate the relationship ill health can have to creativity. We would like to thank our guest editor on this issue, Barbara James, from Women's Health, who joined us to help in its production. Sadly, Catherine Arthur died on 1 December, as we were going to press. We dedicate this issue to her.

Sue O'Sullivan, Alison Read, Lynne Segal, Barbara James

THE SELLING OF HRT: Playing on the Fear Factor

Nancy Worcester and Mariamne H. Whatley

Introduction

For decades, women's health activists have been critical of the medical system's lack of interest in older women's issues. Osteoporosis and heart disease were excellent examples of the problematic relationship between the medical system and women who use it. These prevalent, serious, life-threatening conditions have been characterized by an almost total lack of information and research. Until quite recently, most women had never heard of osteoporosis, and cardiovascular disease was so consistently labelled as a 'men's' disease that the major studies included tens of thousands of men and *no* women.

The situation has changed dramatically in the last few years. Osteoporosis and heart disease can no longer serve as examples of neglect of older women's issues. Osteoporosis has become a household word in the United States. Most women will have seen a headline announcing 'heart disease is the number one killer of women', and the prevention of both osteoporosis and heart disease in women has become 'hot' research.

It might seem that feminist activists should be applauding this response of the medical establishment. Any woman approaching menopause is likely to receive information from her health-care practitioners on the dangers of osteoporosis and heart disease. So why are we complaining? Aren't feminists ever satisfied?

Prevention consciousness
The sudden interest in older women's issues is directly related to the fact that the medical establishment and the drug industry have 'discovered' that healthy menopausal and postmenopausal women

represent a huge market. The selling of hormones and services which promote or follow up on them fits neatly into the needs of the drug industry, as well as health-service providers and consumers. Restrictions by the government and insurance companies in the US have meant the health system cannot make enough money on sick people, and women are not having 'enough' babies; the health system has been forced to search for previously untapped markets of healthy people. Consumers may feel the health system is finally responding to their needs if services and products are marketed to play on their new-found prevention consciousness.

Contemporary US and British societies, especially the middle classes, have become highly health conscious. Advertisements in which bran cereals are pushed to prevent cancer, low cholesterol foods to reduce heart-attack risk, and exercise machines to promote 'wellness' reveal the dominance of the prevention ideology in health awareness. Sometimes the meaning gets sufficiently clouded that it seems that the appearance of health may be an end in itself rather than a means towards a higher-quality life.

The focus on prevention and self-help is part of an overall trend among consumers away from the sick-care model of the medical industry which devotes few resources to environmental and occupational issues, disease detection and control, or medical education, and instead prioritizes drugs, surgery, hospitals and high-technology equipment. This sick-care model may do an impressive job of patching up accident victims or putting a new heart into someone who has eaten the typical high-fat, low-fibre Western diet, but it does practically nothing to keep us well. The initial resistance to the medical model was often political, based, for example, on the analysis generated by the women's health movement; prevention was a way of wrestling control away from doctors and returning it to consumers.

However, it took the medical establishment and others little time to co-opt the emphasis on prevention. This consciousness has been intentionally constructed in a very individualistic, 'take care of *yourself*' (don't expect society, the government or the health system to take care of you) and victim-blaming way. In other words, 'it's the other person's fault if he chooses to live an unhealthy lifestyle'. As major consumers in the health-care system, responsible for their own health and that of other family members, women quickly got targeted as the major customers of prevention services. In her seminars on how to market women's health, Sally Rynne, consultant to for-profit women's health centres throughout the USA, notes that 18 per cent of women's medical visits are preventative, that women are the major subscribers to prevention/wellness type magazines and that the audiences at health-promotion programmes are predominantly women (Whatley and Worcester, 1989). Ironically, although the emphasis on prevention originated as a way to become less dependent on the medical establishment, it is now being used as a marketing technique to attract people back into the system: you cannot prevent osteoporosis or heart disease with HRT without having a doctor's prescription and surrounding services to monitor your 'progress' toward prevention!

Selling the fear factor
In order to maximize the market value of 'prevention', the condition to be avoided must be sufficiently serious or highly undesirable. Individuals must view the condition in question as highly prevalent or believe themselves to have a high level of personal susceptibility. Fear can become an important selling point for either true prevention or early detection tests.

As diseases become 'popular', there is a time of intense interest, during which people are inundated with media coverage of the newest plague, whether it is genital herpes, toxic shock syndrome, premenstrual tension, or chlamydia. Of course, accurate and complete information is needed about these issues; increased awareness is essential for all individuals who want to have some control over their health. However, sensational media coverage often does little besides create fear, as the AIDS panic has clearly demonstrated. Those who benefit from this popular coverage are those who offer prevention or treatment, whether they are effective or not.

The marketing of hormone products to menopausal and postmenopausal women is particularly cruel in the way that it plays on the fears of specific disabling or life-threatening conditions and also, very purposefully, on women's fear of ageing. Disabling or life-threatening conditions are frightening enough in themselves, but ones totally associated with the ageing process, growing older or *being old*, take on an increased meaning for women in an ageist society which particularly devalues older women. It is no coincidence that *Feminine Forever* was the name of the 1966 book which first popularized the notion that a wonder drug (oestrogen) could prevent the ageing process in women.

Swallowing HRT and forgetting its history
Feminine Forever, whose author was funded by Wyeth-Ayerst, the manufacturer of the menopausal oestrogen product Premarin, promised that oestrogen could keep women young forever and prevent the natural 'decaying' process of ageing. It is not surprising that by 1970 Premarin had become one of the top four prescription drugs in the USA (Eagen, 1989). By the mid-1970s, there were cities in the US where more than half of the menopausal women were taking oestrogen (Sloane, 1985). But, by the mid-1970s, studies were starting to show a marked increase in endometrial (lining of the uterus) cancer in women who had taken menopausal oestrogens. While Wyeth-Ayerst denied the oestrogen–endometrial cancer link and even resorted to sending 'Dear Doctor' letters to all gynaecologists in the US (Waterhouse, 1990), women became afraid of the products, doctors feared lawsuits if they prescribed it, and at least another fifteen studies proved that oestrogen use was associated with a marked increase in endometrial cancer (Sloane, 1985). By 1979, a consensus conference of the National Institutes of Health

had rejected almost all claims which had been made for the physical or psychological benefits of oestrogen replacement therapy. The conference committee concluded that of all the presumed symptoms of menopause, there were only two which could be established as uniquely characteristic of menopause and uniformly relieved by oestrogen therapy. Oestrogen is only effective for controlling hot flushes (vasomotor instability) and changes in the genitals (which textbooks refer to as genital atrophy – no wonder women will resort to anything to avoid this condition).

One might think that would be the end of a product which lived up to few of its claims, in which consumers and physicians had lost confidence and which was known as a cancer-causing agent. But, drug companies had tasted the potential of marketing products to menopausal women: in the US more than 28 million prescriptions for oestrogen had been filled in 1975 (National Prescriptions Audit).

The 1980s saw two changes in the marketing of oestrogens: (1) public-relations firms were hired to promote oestrogen products in the same way that sweets, breakfast cereals or soaps are advertised; and (2) oestrogens were reintroduced on to the market in combination with progestins.

Feminist health activists have been critical of the mass marketing of oestrogen products, seeing it as irresponsible. Starting in 1985, Premarin's manufacturer, Wyeth-Ayerst, hired a public-relations firm to conduct a public-education campaign aimed at encouraging *all* women over thirty-five years to consider taking oestrogens to prevent osteoporosis instead of targeting the 25 per cent of women at high risk of suffering osteoporosis. More recently, Ciba Geigy, manufacturer of an oestrogen patch, has begun mass direct-mail solicitations promoting their patch to women throughout the US. Testifying against the mass promotion of oestrogens before the Food and Drug Administration, Cindy Pearson stated, 'The National Women's Health Network is outraged that a potentially risky drug is being promoted with the same techniques used by Publishers Clearinghouse Sweepstakes.' (This refers to the tacky but popular direct-mail selling of magazines by promising highly desirable – but seldom obtainable – prizes) (Pearson, 1991).

By the drug companies' criteria, such promotion of oestrogen products must seem phenomenally successful. In 1985, when Wyeth-Ayerst first started its 'education' campaign on osteoporosis, a survey found that 77 per cent of women had not heard of this condition (Dejanikus, 1985). Now, women have not only heard of osteoporosis, they are also frightened by the seeming inevitability of postmenopausal hip fractures or of becoming like the elderly woman with the severely bent spine they have seen in advertisements. Having dropped to approximately 15 million prescriptions per year in the US in 1979/80, oestrogen prescriptions were up to nearly 32 million in 1989. (National Prescription Audit). Premarin's annual sales alone were put at $400 million by 1989 and expected to exceed $1 billion by 1995. (Waterhouse,

They're as much in love today as they were then...

Later in life, otherwise loving relationships can be marred by atrophic vaginitis. Vagifem delivers local oestrogen and relieves symptoms of dyspareunia and vaginal dryness.[1]

The unique vaginal tablet comes in its slim, single-use applicator and each is individually wrapped. A modern and hygienic alternative to oestrogen creams currently available.

Vagifem for the women of today.

oestradiol
Low Dose, No Mess Therapy for Atrophic Vaginitis

VAGIFEM ABBREVIATED PRESCRIBING INFORMATION
Presentation White vaginal tablet containing 25 micrograms oestradiol USP. Each tablet is inset in a disposable applicator. **Uses** Treatment of atrophic vaginitis due to oestrogen deficiency. **Dosage and Administration** Administered intravaginally using the applicator. The applicator is inserted into the vagina up to the end of the smooth part of the applicator, and the tablet released by pressing the plunger. The applicator is then withdrawn and disposed of. Initial dose of 1 tablet daily for two weeks followed by maintenance dose of 2 tablets per week. Discontinue therapy after about three months to assess need for further therapy. Not intended for children or males. **Contra-indications** Cancer of the breast, uterus and other malignancies believed to be hormone dependent. Undiagnosed abnormal genital bleeding. Pregnancy. Acute thrombophlebitis or thromboembolic disorders associated with oestrogen use. **Precautions** A minor degree of systemic absorption may occur and increased risk of endometrial cancer associated with unopposed oestrogens should be kept in mind. Vaginal infections should be treated before initiation of therapy. Patients with conditions which may be exacerbated by oestrogens should be monitored more frequently and Vagifem treatment withdrawn if the condition worsens. Persistent or recurring vaginal bleeding should be investigated. **Side Effects** Slight vaginal bleeding, vaginal discharge and skin rash have rarely been reported. PL 4668/0026 **PL Holder** Novo Nordisk A/S, Novo Alle, DK 2880 Bagsvaerd, Denmark. **Sole Distributor** Farillon Limited, Ashton Road, Harold Hill, Romford, Essex, RM3 8UE. **Package Quantities and Basic NHS Cost** Cartons containing 15 tablets and applicators = £14.99. **References** 1. Eiermann W. *Proceedings of International Workshop, Copenhagen* 1986; 68-76.

1990). According to federal health statistics, as many as half of all postmenopausal American women take some form of hormone 'replacement' at some time and at least 15 per cent are taking the drugs at any one time (Specter, 1989). This is probably about twice as high as the percentage of British women presently taking menopausal hormones.

Packaging as HRT or ORT

Consumers are now faced with a 'choice' of hormonal products. By the early 1980s oestrogen was often prescribed in combination with a progestin. It was believed that the progestin component would protect against the risk of endometrial cancer which was associated with oestrogen on its own.

For the rest of this paper two different terms will be used to identify the two different forms in which oestrogen is most commonly prescribed. *HRT (hormone replacement therapy)* will be used in reference to products or regimes where a woman is given *both* an oestrogen and a progestin hormone. *ORT (oestrogen replacement therapy)* will be used when a woman is given oestrogen on its own. (Note: because Americans spell oestrogen without a beginning 'o', ERT or estrogen replacement therapy is the term which is used in American publications for oestrogen on its own.) At this stage of the debate about postmenopausal hormones, it is absolutely essential that we keep track of whether we are talking about HRT or ORT.

It is accepted that ORT is related to an increase in endometrial cancer, whereas HRT is not associated with that cancer and may even have a protective effect against endometrial cancer. Any woman with a uterus (in other words women who have not had a hysterectomy) should be informed of this and offered HRT instead of ORT, if HRT is believed to fulfil the purpose for which she is considering hormones. As this paper will discuss, it is a confusing moment in history for women to be making choices about postmenopausal hormones. Most of the studies have been done with ORT, *not* HRT, but a woman with a uterus will want to take HRT. As the studies have not been done, it is simply too early to know whether the progestin component of HRT diminishes or reverses effects expected of oestrogen. As Kathleen MacPherson (1987) points out in her important article 'Osteoporosis: The New Flaw in Woman or Science?', some physicians will not prescribe the HRT combination because: (1) research on its long-term effects is scant, (2) progestins in the contraceptive pills increased the risk of hypertension and strokes, and (3) postmenopausal women may not want to have breakthrough bleeding which occurs monthly if they take the oestrogen-progestin combination.

Women who are considering taking ORT, oestrogen on its own, should be informed that in addition to the approximately five to fourteen-fold increase in endometrial cancer (National Women's Health Network, 1989), women on this regimen also increase their risk of abnormal bleeding 7.8 times, need dilation and curettage 4.9 times as often, and have hysterectomy rates 6.6 times higher, than non-users (Ettinger, 1987). Women who take oestrogens after menopause also have a two to three fold increase in their risk of gallbladder disease (National Women's Health Network, 1989).

Clearly the goal of oestrogen manufacturers is to find a way to package oestrogens so that women are willing to stay on them for their *entire postmenopausal life*:

> We are still learning ways to administer estrogen and progestogen to
> obtain maximum effectiveness with minimum side effects. New
> formulations of estrogens and progestogens, new routes of

administration, and improved dosage schedules should provide more convenient and acceptable long term hormone replacement, one that women can use for their entire postmenopausal life time without the inconvenience of menstrual bleeding and concern about possible side effects. (Ettinger, 1987: 36)

Hormones dominate the system both physiologically and politically

Hormones hold potential for improving quality and quantity of life for some menopausal and postmenopausal women. It will be important to come back to this point and question how feminists can better look at the potential for these hormones. Unfortunately, we seldom have the luxury of being able to do this because major forces are so persistently pushing hormones and because most information is so pro-hormones. In an effort to 'balance' the discussion, feminist health activists have often ended up as lone voices critiquing the premature, routine prescribing of these drugs of unknown safety.

Even if women have *all* the available information on postmeno-pausal hormones, with the present state of knowledge it is extremely difficult to weigh the potential benefits and the unknown risks. But, in fact, very few women 'choosing' to embark upon hormone treatment even know that the drugs they are taking are controversial and possibly hazardous. The information women get in the lay press is very much biased towards the use of hormones. A survey of all the articles on this topic in the magazines most regularly read by US women found that thirty-six articles were published between 1985 and 1988. Three-quarters of the articles were clearly pro-hormones: fully half of the articles did not even mention any risks with oestrogen use (Pearson, 1991). The information women get from their doctors may be nearly as biased: a 1990 study found that over 75 per cent of US gynaecologists were routinely prescribing hormones to prevent osteoporosis or heart disease in all menopausal women.

Even the smallest doses of ORT or HRT have very powerful effects on a woman's body and totally dominate her body's own regulation and production of hormones. How desirable or safe this is physiologically is a question which is still unanswered. What is known is that the way hormones are being promoted now has dangerous political implications for women and must be seen as part of a purposeful medicalization of women's lives.

Feminists have long been critical of the ways in which normal, healthy processes such as contraception, pregnancy and childbirth have been medicalized. We used to criticize the fact that real health issues such as premenstrual tension, infertility, and osteoporosis were ignored by the health system. Now that women's health issues have been 'discovered' and there are money-making drugs or technologies to offer, we see a medicalization of whole new areas of women's lives. We are already witnessing what this means. The medical profession is taking control over more aspects of women's lives, more conditions are being labelled as illness and used against the equality of women, drugs or high technology procedures have been identified as the solution to newly targeted 'problems' and, in the name of prevention, more women are being hooked into a medical system which does not meet their needs.

The medicalization of menopause means that menopause and postmenopause are defined as 'deficiency illnesses'. Even the terms 'hormone replacement therapy' and 'oestrogen replacement therapy' wrongly imply that something is missing which must be replaced. The fact that this misinformation can so easily be used as a selling point for products is a sad reflection on how little information most women have about their own bodies. As the National Women's Health Network's position paper on hormone therapy puts it, 'We object to the view of normal menopause as a deficiency disease. Menopause does not automatically require "treatment".' (National Women's Health Network, 1989: 9)

Menopause is a normal, healthy transition phase of a woman's life when her body has within it all the mechanisms necessary to gradually change from dealing with demanding reproductive cycles to meeting the different, postreproduction, physiological needs of postmenopause. The postmenopausal woman is still capable of making the oestrogens she needs: the older woman's body needs less oestrogen and makes it in a different way. During the reproductive years, a woman's ovaries will be the main producers of oestrogens and relatively high quantities of oestrogens will be produced. Menopause is the time when the ovaries gradually stop producing oestrogens and the oestrogens produced by the adrenal glands and the oestrogens produced from androgens by fat and muscle tissue become the major oestrogens in a woman's body. Menopause should be viewed as the healthy transition from premenopause to postmenopause in the same way that puberty is recognized as the time when young women make the transition from prereproduction to being capable of reproduction.

Viewing menopause as a normal, healthy transition does not imply that transition is easy for all women. Although many of the problems faced by menopausal women are social rather than physiological, women may experience symptoms such as hot flushes when or if their oestrogen levels drop rapidly (which is what happens if a woman's ovaries are surgically removed). Taking ORT or HRT works to *delay* the transition by keeping hormone levels artificially high. If a woman suddenly stops taking hormones she can experience the same or worse symptoms than the ones for which she was taking hormones. If a woman chooses to take ORT or HRT to relieve hot flushes or genital changes, to *ease* the transition she would want to take gradually reduced amounts of hormones for as short a period of time as possible for specific complaints (National Women's Health Network, 1989: 9).

The medicalization of menopause is particularly dangerous in that *all* attention has become focused on hormones as the 'answer' to whatever is identified as the menopausal/postmenopausal 'problem'. While some women may benefit from hormones, many or most women will be able to go through the transition phase and minimize osteo-porosis and heart-disease risks with less hazardous measures such as a healthy diet, appropriate physical exercise, and using alternatives to hormones. Whether in determining research priorities or influencing the information the mass media should give to empower women through informed decision-making, much more attention needs to be focused on healthy alternatives to hormones. As Kathleen MacPherson (1987: 60) puts it:

> To recommend widespread use of HRT as a public health measure to prevent osteoporosis without assessing the needs of individual women would be the same as recommending that everyone take antihypertensive drugs because so many people have high blood pressure. For no other condition is anything as potentially dangerous as hormones being recommended as a preventative measure.

Osteoporosis

Creating the fear of osteoporosis
In order to create markets for their products, both drug companies and calcium manufacturers effectively used the media to introduce people to osteoporosis, a previously ignored condition, and to scare them into buying products which promised to prevent this. Both prevention consciousness and fear of ageing contributed to the success of osteo-porosis-related advertising. Many advertisements played on both of these, such as one for a calcium supplement which showed a healthy thirty-year-old transformed to a stooped 65-year-old within thirty seconds (Giges, 1986). Such an image not only capitalizes on the fear of losing youthful attractiveness, it also draws on even deeper fears of disability leading to loss of independence. Information on hip fractures has been presented in an even more frightening way. For example, a popular guide to preventing osteoporosis states: 'The consequences of hip fractures can be devastating. Fewer than one-half of all women who suffer a hip fracture regain normal function. Fifteen percent die shortly after their injury, and nearly 30 percent die within a year' (Notelovitz and Ware, 1982: 37). The deaths are not inevitable and are related to complications such as pneumonia but they certainly serve as a useful scare tactic.

The information about complications of osteoporosis as a major 'killer' of women in their eighties and the linking of osteoporosis with menopause in such a way that osteoporosis practically becomes identi-fied as a symptom of menopause, can be further connected to imply that menopause itself is a killer unless hormones are taken to stop this process.

In fact, osteoporosis and how it affects people, is much more complicated and unpredictable than the hormone- and calcium-promoting information suggests. Osteoporosis is not an 'all or nothing' condition, it is 'not a disease like tuberculosis that a person either has or does not have' (Parfitt, 1984). A statement like, 'It would appear inevitable that if a person lives long enough, he or she will suffer from osteoporosis.' (Kirkpatrick, 1987: 45) may help British or American women put their newly created fear of osteoporosis into perspective. However, taking a more cross-cultural approach such as, 'osteoporosis is not a natural part of ageing and does not occur all over the world, even among the elderly' (Brown, 1988) will be more useful for understanding that osteoporosis is not inevitable, is very much related to industrial-ized/Western diets and lifestyles, and that *real* prevention has nothing to do with hormones.

> Looking at cross-cultural data, we see that blaming osteoporosis on an estrogen deficiency is just a little less absurd than blaming heart attacks on a deficiency of by-pass surgery. Surgery might solve the problem for a while, but it is not a deficiency of the operation that caused the problem. (Brown, 1988: 6)

Osteoporosis often gets billed as a major health issue for all older women, when, in fact, some women are much more at risk than others. The fact that lighter complexioned women with ancestors from northern Europe or Asia are much more likely to develop osteoporosis than darker complexioned women with African, Hispanic, Mediterranean or Native American ancestry probably accounts for this condition finally receiving the attention it has. Pressing health needs of 'minority' older women as defined by the women themselves still tend to get ignored. While looking at ethnic influence on osteoporosis risk, several other points should be made. The osteoporosis risk for Jewish women seems to lie somewhere between the relatively low or relatively high risks of the above mentioned groups. The term 'Black' is used differently in American and British publications. So, while it is accurate to say Black (meaning African-American) women are less at risk than white women in the US, in the British context, it must be clarified that women of Asian descent will be at significantly higher risk than women of African ancestry. Also, just because groups have lower rates of osteoporosis, does not mean that no one in those groups is at risk. Good health information materials need to emphasize this (Partlow, 1991).

Fractures are not synonymous with osteoporosis
Similarly, the disabling or life-threatening fractures must not be seen as synonymous with osteoporosis. Not all women with osteoporosis have fractures, not all women with fractures have osteoporosis. Studies have shown that women with and without hip fractures had similar bone densities, and women in other cultures have low rates of bone fractures even with low bone density (National Women's Health Network, 1989).
Factors such as tendency to fall, muscle strength, flexibility, having to walk on icy pavements, etc., will influence the chance of fracture as

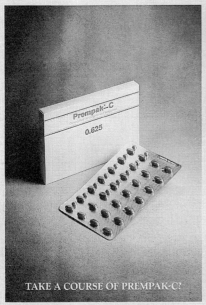
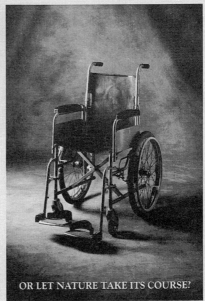
much as the density of bone mass (Whatley, 1988a). Falls in the elderly are known to be significantly greater for people using antidepressants, sedative/hypnotics and vasodilators (drugs that dilate blood vessels) (Myers, 1991) and modification of medications has been shown to be an effective method of reducing falls and fractures in a nursing-home setting (Wolfe, 1991a). So in many cases, reducing rather than increasing

drugs will be the key preventative issue for minimizing complications of osteoporosis in elderly women.

A more creative and caring, less profit-motivated approach might come up with some very interesting ideas about what to do about osteoporosis (Whatley, 1988a). For example, Kathleen MacPherson emphasizes that health policies must reflect the need for bold structural changes in our society instead of the usual incremental or 'bandaid' policies suggested as osteoporosis prevention (MacPherson, 1987: 61). Her recommendations are for policies 'to alleviate the feminization of poverty, a living wage, pension plans, social security benefits for homemakers, etc, and a national health care plan to provide ongoing health promotion and maintenance for all citizens.'

Although studies have shown that ORT can slow down bone loss and can reduce the risk of hip fractures, that information gets misinterpreted into inaccurate messages. ORT may slow down bone loss but it does nothing to restore bone mineral (Ettinger, 1987), but how many women with osteoporosis are informed that the most ORT can do for them is to slow down or stabilize their condition? Many women who are taking HRT are making that decision based upon what is known about ORT. A few studies have shown that HRT also helps slow down bone loss, but no study has shown a reduction in fractures in women taking HRT (National Women's Health Network, 1989).

Osteoporosis screening
Detecting osteoporosis also gets deliberately confused with preventing the condition. In the US, osteoporosis screening has been widely promoted. Finding a noninvasive way to predict a woman's risk for fractures may seem a benefit of medical science with which few could find fault. Certainly the prevalence and potential consequences of osteoporosis are serious enough to justify screening.

However, an evaluation of bone mass measurements as a screening procedure reveals a different picture (Napoli, 1988 and Whatley and Worcester, 1989). Several techniques are currently being used to detect osteoporosis and these techniques vary in availability, cost, accuracy, reproducibility, and what they actually measure. But, there are certain problems with all of them and the most available techniques are the least reliable.

While screening can show that bone mass has been lost, screening cannot predict how rapidly someone will be losing bone and cannot predict whether or not someone is at risk from osteoporosis. Bone loss is neither constant nor predictable. Knowing someone's bone mass at one age does not help predict how fast that woman will lose bone mass; a woman with a low bone mass may end up losing at a very slow rate and a woman with a much higher bone mass might end up losing rapidly (Whatley, 1988a). Screening is even limited in its ability to identify full-blown cases of the disease. While bone density screening would be expected to differentiate between those who do and do not have osteoporosis-related hip fractures, these measurements are of little use in the most at-risk elderly population because, 'if the highest bone mass seen in patients with fractures is designated as the "fracture threshold", then nearly all women over seventy will by definition have osteoporosis' (Ott, 1986: 875).

It must be emphasized that techniques for measuring bone mass are extremely useful for research purposes. However, at this stage, unreliable but sophisticated, expensive screening has little to offer the consumer. Requiring regular monitoring of bone mass, osteoporosis screening offers enormous potential for clinics as a profitable procedure. There is also the possibility that women will be hooked into a system which has little to offer them except hormone prescriptions and the advice that weight-bearing exercises and a calcium-rich diet at an earlier age 'might have helped' (Worcester and Whatley, 1988a).

Role of diet

Indeed, there is plenty of evidence that Western/industrialized life-styles and diets are responsible for the prevalence of osteoporosis and the fact that it affects women much more than men. Britain and the US report much higher rates of osteoporosis than less industrialized/ Westernized countries. For example, the US rate is 24 times higher than that of some other countries. People in Singapore, Hong Kong, certain parts of Yugoslavia and the Maori of New Zealand have very low rates of osteoporosis-caused fractures, and Africans and people living tra-ditional lifestyles have been described as 'almost immune' to osteo-porosis (Brown, 1988).

Osteoporosis as a male disease in Britain and the US gets very little attention (because no one has figured out how to convince men that their problems are all due to 'oestrogen deficiency'?) despite the fact that (US) men suffer one-sixth as many spinal fractures and approximately one-half as many hip fractures as women. In other parts of the world, in Hong Kong, some parts of Yugoslavia, and in the South African Bantu, it has been documented that men experience osteoporosis and fractures at the same or higher rates than women. Medical anthropologist Susan Brown (1988) gives the following explanations for the excessive develop-ment of osteoporosis in Western women: (1) as a group, women have less exposure to sunlight which helps the body make vitamin D which is essential for calcium absorption; (2) women are not encouraged to be as physically active; (3) women use more prescription drugs; (4) women are more subject to removal of the sex-hormone producing gonads, the ovaries (if the testes are removed, men also develop osteoporosis); and (5) men generally consume a higher-quality/more nutritional diet than women.

Western diets contribute to the development of osteoporosis both by not providing enough calcium in the first place, and more importantly, by 'wasting' the calcium which is ingested. The typical Western diet encourages a heavy imbalance in the ratio of phosphorus (high levels in carbonated beverages and high-protein foods, including meats) to calcium which can cause a loss of bone calcium; low levels of vitamin D and high levels of fibre, oxalates and phytates interfere with calcium absorption and high intakes of caffeine and alcohol also significantly contribute to excessive bone loss (Finn, 1987 and Brown, 1988). Instead of dealing with anything as complex as the calcium-wasting effects of our diet, or questioning reducing foods like meat which are central to our diet and economy, calcium has been promoted as something one can simply add to what one already consumes. Retail sales of calcium supplements grew from $18 million in 1980 to $166 million in 1986, a calcium-fortified sugar-free drink mix was marketed, and the sales of the diet cola, Tab, tripled when calcium was added. Jumping on the calcium bandwagon and hoping it would make people forget their cholesterol concern, the dairy industry launched a campaign with the theme 'dairy foods: calcium the way nature intended' (Giges, 1986).

It is well established that because bone mass peaks at age thirty-five years, the greatest benefit from calcium occurs in the years from birth to age thirty-five (Finn, 1987). However, it is discouraging to see how, in the push towards hormones, the role of calcium for menopausal and postmenopausal women has been ignored or discounted. In explaining why recommended intakes of calcium for older women had not been increased in the Food and Nutrition Board's latest (10th edition) *Recommendation for Daily Nutrient Allowances*, the director stated, 'because oestrogen is more effective in preventing osteoporosis than calcium'.

That answer is much too simplistic and totally ignores the risks of oestrogens and the fact that many women cannot or will not take hormones. Most importantly, such attitudes influence research and policy agendas so that the potential of calcium alone or in sufficient quantities to reduce the amounts of oestrogens needed, is not being explored despite work showing the merit of this approach. In a study believed to be the first to look at both lifelong and current calcium intake in normal postmenopausal women not taking oestrogens, researchers found a protective effect of calcium on bone density in women who reported high calcium intakes *both* throughout their lifetime and presently (Cauley, 1988). Even Bruce Ettinger, previously quoted as supporting the goal of keeping women on oestrogens for their entire postmenopausal lives, gives us reason to believe calcium deserves more attention. He states:

> Although calcium given alone is incapable of maintaining skeletal mass, high intakes of calcium allow estrogen to be more effective; by simply augmenting calcium intake to 1,500 mg. per day, women may be adequately protected while taking half the usual dosage of estrogen . . . It has also been suggested but not proven that very low intake of calcium – perhaps less than 300 mg. per day – can also diminish or abolish estrogen's protection (Ettinger, 1987: 33–4).

Thinking of *real* osteoporosis prevention is a useful case study of how lifelong interactions of social, economic and political issues affect women's health and how factors in a young woman's life affect her chances of being able to maximize on her full potential. With 'femininity' so closely associated with an obsession with thinness and conflicting messages given to young women about physical activity, sex-role socialization and gender identity have to be seen as causal agents of osteoporosis. The obsession with thinness and fear of fat promote osteoporosis in several different ways. First, avoiding high-calcium foods because of calorific content, dieting that results in nutritional deficiencies or nutritional imbalances, fasting and purging can be identified as behaviours which interfere with calcium absorption and contribute to low peak bone mass (Kirkpatrick, 1987). Secondly, low body weight reduces the mechanical forces applied to the skeleton by gravity and muscle contraction so there is less 'built-in' stimulation for bone formation. As a generalization, heavier people tend towards more bone mass (Goodman, 1987). Additionally, it is well established that fat tissue in a woman's body produces oestrogen and the more fat a woman has, the more oestrogen she will produce. But how many women know this or can listen to the message if they hear it? Society so consistently pushes thinness and hormones, that contradictory healthy advice like Mary Kirkpatrick's 'A Self Care Model for Osteoporosis' is seldom mentioned.

> Ironically, midlife may be a good time to have a little extra weight to act as a protective mechanism against osteoporosis. If fat tissue provides more estrogen, the bone loss at menopause may be slowed. Also, body weight can act as a loading factor and can produce necessary stress on the bony structure to form bone mass. (Kirkpatrick, 1987: 48–9).

Physical activity

Numerous studies have shown that exercise, particularly of the weight-bearing type, can promote bone strength in women under thirty-five and help maintain bone mass in women over thirty-five. But, how often do women, particularly young women, get useful, sensible advice about the health benefits of moderate exercise? Too often women get only one of two equally inappropriate messages: don't exercise or, do too much of it!

When tested for physical performance, girls and boys are matched up to ages ten to twelve. Thereafter, they get very different messages about what is 'ladylike' or 'masculine' and, after age twelve, boys tend to increase in strength and cardiovascular fitness more than girls who are discouraged from being physically active (Whatley, 1988b). The young women who resist the pressure to be sedentary, are often encouraged to go to the other extreme. Both the 'cosmetic athletes' who obsessively exercise to achieve 'beauty' and the serious athletes who exercise too strenuously, can delay menarche or cause amenorrhoea which can be detrimental to building bone density (Goodman, 1987).

Interestingly, the relationship of 'athletic amenorrhoea' to osteoporosis started attracting quite a bit of media attention as more young women have begun to explore their athletic capabilities. Physio-logically, the explanation and consequences of amenorrhoea may be the same whether caused by athletic training, ballet dancing or extreme dieting. However, as Western cultures find ballet and dieting to be ideal 'feminine' activities, the media attention has focused almost exclusively on the potential osteoporotic risks of athletic amenorrhoea. Regular, moderate, weight-bearing exercise is undoubtedly a healthier approach to osteoporosis prevention. Further research is needed to determine the type, intensity, duration and frequency of physical activity which best builds and maintains bone mass (Goodman, 1987).

When to start hormones?
If one believes that hormone therapy is the way to prevent osteoporosis, when should that be started?

The peak of bone mass is reached by the time a person reaches thirty-five. After that, both men and women will gradually lose minerals from their bone for the rest of their lives. Menopause gets associated with this process because women lose bone mass most rapidly during the transition years immediately before, during, and after menopause. Susan Brown (1988) explains that, 'a woman loses a full half of all the bone she will lose during her lifetime between the age of thirty-five and fifty.' Jessop McDonnell (1987: 11) states it less delicately: 'the eight to ten years following menopause may be characterized by a ravaging assault on the skeletal system.' When a woman has settled into being postmenopausal, the rate of bone loss will slow down to being similar to the rate at which men have been losing minerals.

The years thirty-five to fifty are key years for prevention. Ettinger emphasizes:

> Correct timing and adequate duration of estrogen therapy can maximize
> the therapy's benefits. Women should begin taking estrogen at
> menopause; the longer they delay, the less bone protection will be
> obtained. Knowing that the most rapid phase of bone loss is in the five to
> ten years after menopause, most experts do not recommend estrogen for
> postmenopausal women who have not taken estrogen during the first 10
> to 15 years after the onset of menopause. (1987: 36).

Obvious problems become apparent. Many women being screened for osteoporosis *are* being started on hormones well after they would have had their most benefit. This can create a 'yo-yo' effect as the body adjusts to postmenopausal levels of oestrogen, then must readjust to artificially high levels. Not being told how hormones work, many women go on and off hormones without realizing that the 'yo-yo' effect could actually exaggerate loss of bone. Once women are on hormones, they will need to stay on them indefinitely, to keep delaying the transition which would cause loss of bone. The ramifications, of course, are that women are on hormones from premenopause for the rest of their lives and dependent upon expensive medical services to monitor how their bodies adjust to these products. A drug would have to have minimal side effects to be appropriate for continuous use for this duration of time. In fact, beginning on oestrogen during perimenopausal years and continuing for many years is exactly the pattern of use which puts women most at risk for breast cancer. With that information, many women will feel that their own risk of osteoporosis does not justify the increased risk of breast cancer.

Heart disease

Women may have become saturated with information about ORT and osteoporosis; a new angle has been necessary to raise anxiety to the point at which a new group of women will actively seek ORT prescriptions. The long overdue attention to *prevention* of heart disease in women has provided exactly the right focus for an expanded ORT market, giving physicians an additional rationale to prescribe it. The new media coverage of women and heart disease has helped generate fears and then ORT has been offered as the solution.

This contrasts with approaches in the past when very little attention had been paid to either prevention or treatment of heart disease in women, for it has traditionally been viewed as a man's disease. While men experience heart disease at younger ages and have more heart attacks than women, women account for 47 per cent of the heart-attack deaths in the United States, making it the leading cause of death for women (Winslow, 1991). In addition, women who suffer a heart attack are more likely to die than men (39 per cent vs 31 per cent) and more likely to suffer a second heart attack within four years (20 per cent vs 15 per cent) (Winslow, 1991). However, these high risks for women have not been reflected in treatment. For example, in one study of patients hospitalized for coronary heart disease, men were 28 per cent more likely to have angiography, a procedure to determine the extent of arterial blockage, and 48 per cent more likely to have bypass surgery or balloon angioplasty. In another study of men and women hospitalized for major heart attacks, men were nearly twice as likely to have angiography and bypass surgery (Winslow, 1991). This study also found that, before the heart attack, chest pains and other symptoms were more disabling for women than men. One of the authors of the latter report emphasized her concern that women who continued to have chest pains after their heart attacks still do not receive angiography (Kolata, 1991a).

These studies and others document the lack of attention by the medical profession to heart disease as a major women's health issue, but the fact that these studies exist at all is a sign that there is finally some concern. If heart disease is the leading killer of women in the United States, why has there been so little emphasis on it before? Why do so many women fear breast cancer but are apparently unaware of their risks of heart disease? Without going into reasons for past neglect, it is possible to offer some explanations for the new-found hype of heart disease as 'number 1 killer of women'. One view is that the market is fickle and there needs to be a 'disease of the month' to capture the interest of the media, consumers, practitioners, and the people (politicians included) who control research funding. However, with an old disease, only a new angle, preferably with something to sell, will generate the necessary interest. For example, there was considerable media attention when a study suggested that aspirin reduced the risk of heart attacks in men (Steering Committee of the Physicians' Health Study Group, 1989). Aspirin manufacturers must have been delighted by the press aspirin received, especially after the earlier negative publicity about Reye syndrome, a potentially fatal condition in children caused by aspirin being given during a viral infection such as flu or chicken-pox. However, the media reports rarely mentioned that the study was done on men only and could not be extrapolated to women. In response to the gap in the research, a recent study reported that women who took one to six aspirin a week experienced a 25 per cent reduction in risk of heart attack compared to women who took no aspirin (Manson, Stampfer, and Colditz, 1991). The results are hardly conclusive, however. The study, which included only nurses, was an observational one, not an experimental one (the women made their own choices about taking aspirin and reported their choices. The researchers simply looked for the effects). This leads to the strong possibility of confounding variables, for the groups may vary in much more than the factor of aspirin use (Appel and Bush, 1991).

In spite of the flaws, this study received a lot of publicity and generated more interest in women and heart disease, providing a good opening for calling attention to the role of ORT in preventing heart disease. In an apparent attempt to expand their market, Wyeth-Ayerst, the manufacturers of Premarin, the most commonly prescribed oral oestrogen, requested that the US Food and Drug Administration (FDA) allow promotion of Premarin for the prevention of heart disease, at least for women who have had hysterectomies (Rovner, 1990). The FDA Advisory Committee concluded, after listening to much conflicting testimony, that 'the cardiovascular benefits of estrogen replacement therapy with Premarin in women without a uterus may outweigh the risks, considering the individual patient's risk for various estrogen-related diseases and conditions' (Rovner, 1990: 9). Dangerously, this statement, as it has been reported and repeated, has been reduced to a simple 'benefits outweigh the risks'; in addition, the distinctions between ORT and HRT are rarely clarified.

In terms of the research itself, the results are not clear-cut. Generalizations are limited because almost all the subjects have been white and middle class. As with the aspirin study, these studies have been observational; the researchers did not control the choice of treatments but merely observed the results based on the women's choices. A major confounding factor is that the women who *choose* Premarin may be at reduced risk for heart attack anyway. For example, a co-author of the major lipid study cited in the FDA hearings, Elizabeth Barrett-Connor, said that women who used Premarin were also less likely to smoke, were thinner, and were better educated than non-users, all of which might have been factors in reducing risk (Rovner, 1990). One of the clearest ways to emphasize that users and non-users may represent different populations is the result of one study which found users of oestrogen had lower mortality rates, not only from heart disease, but also from accidents, suicide and homicide. As Cindy Pearson, of the National Women's Health Network, asked, when she was testifying *against* FDA approval for Premarin being promoted for the prevention of heart disease, 'Does this mean we can conclude that estrogen use protects one from being murdered?' (Rovner, 1990: 9).

No study completed to date has been without the major flaw of lack of comparability between users and non-users of ORT. This is well illustrated in a study published after the FDA hearings, which was heralded as more good news about ORT. The study of 49,000 post-menopausal women showed 44 per cent fewer heart attacks and 39 per cent reduced risk of heart-attack death in those who took ORT (Kolata, 1991b). However, the study was on nurses, 98 per cent of whom were white, who had made their own choices about use of ORT. As an example of this problem, a very heavy woman, who might be more at risk for heart attack, might also be less likely to select ORT because she would also be *less* likely to experience menopausal changes for which ORT is recommended. A nurse who considered herself at risk for heart disease might not have taken ORT because physicians in the 1970s were discouraging women at risk of heart disease from taking oestrogen at all (Sojourner, 1991).

Besides the studies directed at heart-attack risks, much of the support for the role of ORT in preventing heart disease comes from data on HDL (high density lipoprotein) and LDL (low density lipoprotein). *Higher* HDL and *lower* LDL are favourable to reduced risk of heart disease. A review article by Bush and colleagues (Bush *et al.*, 1988) provides a good summary of the factors affecting these lipoproteins in women. These include genetics, diet, obesity, exercise, alcohol, cigarette smoking, oral contraceptives.

The data on oral contraceptives is particularly interesting. All formulations increase LDL, the 'bad lipoprotein'. The largest increases in LDL occur with the lowest oestrogen dose and the strongest anti-oestrogenic progestin. As the potency of progestin increases, HDL, the 'good' lipoprotein, decreases. The implications from the oral-contraceptive data for the use of ORT as compared to HRT are borne out by the studies on oestrogens as menopausal therapy. According to Bush and colleagues (Bush *et al.*, 1988), use of unopposed and synthetic oestrogens leads to the more favourable HDL/LDL profile. However, cyclic oestrogen-progestin therapy (HRT) has either a minimal or adverse effect on lipoproteins, depending on the progestin used. In other words, while oestrogen therapy by itself may have very positive effects, the addition of progestins completely negates those effects. HRT, therefore, in the best case, provides no benefits in terms of HDL/LDL profile, the main route by which ORT is believed to have a protective effect against heart disease. However, many women take HRT to avoid the increased risks from ORT in terms of endometrial cancer. If the progestin component protects against endometrial cancer but undoes the protective effects against heart disease, women may have to make difficult decisions about which disease they fear most.

The lipoprotein data also provides some interesting results about alcohol. Bush *et al.* (1988) state that moderate alcohol consumption is strongly related to increased HDL levels in men and women. A recent report suggested that moderate alcohol consumption has a protective effect against heart disease in men, which supports previous work finding benefits for men and women. If oestrogen manufacturers are allowed to say their products reduce heart disease, why shouldn't beer and wine companies request that the FDA allow them to promote their products as reducing risk of heart disease? Such a claim would surely be countered with the argument that the risks of alcohol consumption outweigh the benefits. But do we really know that benefits of ORT outweigh the risks?

Some of the answers about ORT and HRT may come from a new study known as PEPI, the Postmenopausal Estrogen/Progestin Interventions Trial, which is funded by the National Institutes of Health. It is a double-blinded placebo study, with random assignment of women to one of five groups: oestrogen only, one of three oestrogen/progestin combinations, or placebo only. The study will measure, among other factors, cholesterol and its fractions, and blood pressure, while also studying osteoporosis and endometrial changes. When the data from this study is analysed completely, it may be appropriate to make some recommendations about HRT and ORT. Unfortunately, the study is only for three years so only short-term consequences can be evaluated. We may know something more about short-term changes in HDL, LDL, and bone density. However, information about other risks, especially breast cancer, will not be forthcoming.

In the meantime, while we wait for the data to come in, perhaps it would be more appropriate to focus on what we do know about preventing heart disease in women and provide education about diet, exercise, smoking, and treating high blood pressure (Wolfe, 1991b).

Breast cancer

In the attempt to reduce the risk of heart disease or osteoporosis by taking ORT or HRT, women may be replacing one disease with another. There is strong evidence that oestrogens increase the risk of breast cancer, but the issue seems to be how big a risk that really is. A Swedish study, published in 1989, showed a 10 per cent increased relative risk of breast cancer in women on oestrogens, with the risk increasing with length of treatment. After nine years of use, there was an excess risk of

70 per cent. The addition of progestins did not reduce the risk and may even have increased it slightly (Bergkvist *et al.*, 1989). The differences in the oestrogen of choice in the US and Sweden was apparently one reason why this study did not receive more press, as well as the fact that the risk was seen as only slightly increased.

A later study from the United States received more attention but also was presented as showing a slight risk. In a study that followed over 12,000 nurses for ten years, Colditz and colleagues found that women taking oestrogen were 30 to 40 per cent more likely to develop breast cancer than those who did not (Colditz *et al.*, 1990). This might be seen as a serious risk in a disease which may strike one out of nine women in the United States. However, the media coverage played down the effects as slight. For example, referring to the increased risk of 30 to 40 per cent, one article claimed, 'But this risk is considered small; it is only about half the risk a woman faces if her mother had breast cancer' (Kolata, 1990: A11). This is hardly reassuring for women considering ORT who have other risk factors, particularly the woman whose mother had breast cancer. The one note that women may actually find reassuring is that the additional risk seems to disappear a year after stopping oestrogens. However, that does not help women much who are on a long-term plan for oestrogen to maintain reduced risk of osteoporosis and heart disease.

A large number of studies on ORT and breast cancer were evaluated using meta-analysis, a statistical method to evaluate data from a number of studies, which can give a more accurate picture than a single study (Steinberg *et al.*, 1991). The data suggests an increased risk of breast cancer for women who used oestrogen for more than five years. Women with a family history of breast cancer had a markedly increased risk. A particularly interesting finding was that the studies in which oestrogen therapy was started before menopause showed a much greater increase in risk than those which included only women who started oestrogen after menopause. Because oestrogen as a prevention for osteoporosis should ideally be started *before* menopause to prevent the period of greatest bone loss, those women who follow the plan most likely to prevent osteoporosis will be at most risk for breast cancer. They will have started before menopause and they will need to continue indefinitely, because if they go off at any time the bone loss will occur quickly. The duration of oestrogen therapy is clearly related to risk and going off it seems the only way to reduce the risk. While progestins may protect these women against endometrial cancer, it will apparently do nothing to reduce breast-cancer risks.

In weighing up the risks of breast cancer versus the possibility that ORT or HRT can prevent osteoporosis or heart disease, women essentially need to decide which disease they fear the most. Dr Lynn Rosenberg, a Boston epidemiologist, says that most women decide whether to take oestrogen by a sort of fear meter, asking themselves which diseases or discomforts they most dread (Kolata, 1991c). Even more to the point, Dr Adrienne Fugh-Berman (1991: 3), speaking on behalf of the National Women's Health Network puts it:

We are concerned that the concept of disease prevention may be expanded to include the concept of disease substitution.

Dr Fugh-Berman's statement was made in reference to tamoxifen, a totally different topic, but one which we mention here for the purpose of emphasizing the complications and unknowns of menopausal/ postmenopausal hormones. Tamoxifen is a drug which has been recognized for its effectiveness in prolonging the disease-free interval in postmenopausal women with oestrogen receptor-positive breast cancer. However, now, tamoxifen is being experimented with in both England and the US as a way to *prevent* breast cancer in normal healthy women. In the US, the National Women's Health Network was the only organization to present testimony to the Food and Drug Administration Committee on Oncology Drugs opposing the trial. This is not the place to detail why the trial is 'premature in its assumptions, weak in its hypotheses, questionable in its ethics, and misguided in its public health ramifications' (Fugh-Berman, 1991: 3). Relevant to this paper is the fact that taxomifen is known to be effective as breast-cancer treatment because it works as an *anti*-oestrogen: it blocks the effect of oestrogen on the breast. Researchers justify studying the effects of tamoxifen on healthy women because they feel there is sufficient evidence to suggest that blocking the effects of oestrogen on the breasts may be a way of preventing (delaying?) breast cancer.

The irony of the situation is obvious. How can it be that at this particular moment in history, in the name of 'prevention', huge numbers of women are being given oestrogen products and another group is being studied with anti-oestrogens? *All* the women taking either oestrogens or anti-oestrogens are part of massive experiments which should help us learn more about hormones but do *nothing* to support health-promoting methods of disease prevention.

Conclusion

HRT raises large questions for individual women trying to decide whether to take it and for women's health movements which must analyse why, once again, huge numbers of women are swallowing a product of unknown safety. There are no simple answers for either individual women or for feminist health activists.

Many of the issues which individual women will want to weigh as they make their own decisions have been covered in this paper. At some level, it is a very personal decision to balance known and unknown risks with the narrow range of choices available. Each woman will want to make today's and tomorrow's decisions based on her own personal hormone history. Most of the studies which have been done have been on women for whom oral contraceptives were not available. It remains to be seen how much different formulations of oral contraceptives for different lengths of time influence issues related to ORT or HRT. Much research will be done on many aspects of hormone use in the next few years. Any woman taking, or considering, hormones should find a source of information which she trusts, such as Women's Health in England or the National Women's Health Network in North America. Excellent health check-ups, including pelvic exams, mammography and physical breast exams, pap smears, monitoring of blood lipids and blood pressure, and endometrial biopsies, must be available to all women who are or have been on hormones for any length of time.

HRT raises enormous challenges for women's health movements. Many of us have lived through the tragedies of DES daughters, the Dalkon Shield, thalidomide, and toxic shock syndrome. One of the biggest questions must be, why aren't the lessons from the immediate past more central to our present debates? Why do large numbers of women not know about, or choose to ignore, the tremendous risks involved in taking drugs whose long-term safety is not known? An even trickier question is why are so few people questioning the long-term safety of hormonal products for menopausal and postmenopausal women? A number of people who have been allies in the struggle for safer contraceptives are not involved in evaluating and critiquing the mass marketing of ORT and HRT. Is ageism a factor? Are we willing to accept a few more side effects in a product designed specifically for older women? Are we willing to lower our standards just a wee bit for products which promise to interfere with the ageing process?

The HRT debate – or more accurately, the *lack* of debate – serves as a reminder of the urgency of empowering *all* women to understand their own bodies and for them to have access to appropriate (language, reading level, relevant to own issues) information for the 'choices' they face. One of the biggest lessons in the marketing of HRT has been that many women still do not know enough about the normal healthy workings of their bodies to resist a mass manipulation of the fear factor.

ORT and HRT are valuable products. Their availability will definitely make a difference in the quality and length of life for *some* women. However, they will probably never be products which should be given to *most* women for a long length of time. If these products are as valuable as the manufacturers say, they should be available to the women who would benefit most from them. In the present situation it tends to be the healthiest groups of women with easy access to the medical system who are given hormones.

To answer any of the questions raised in this paper, long-term, controlled studies which look at multiple parameters and the inter-actions of many factors must be done with diverse groups of women. Without a clearer understanding of the actual value and risks of ORT and HRT, the mass marketing of these products is certainly premature. A renewed focus on *real* prevention and self-help as a way of wrestling control *for* the consumer, *away* from the medical system and makers of highly profitable products, continues to be an urgent priority for women's health movements.

Notes

Nancy Worcester and Mariamne H. Whatley teach women's health courses in the Women's Studies Program at the University of Wisconsin-Madison and are editors of *Women's Health: Readings on Social, Economic and Political Issues*.

Nancy was a founding member of the Women's Health Information Centre in London and has been on the National Women's Health Network Board since 1986. She is the Women's Studies Outreach Specialist for UW-Madison.

Mariamne is associate chair of the UW-Madison Women's Studies Program and directs the Health Education Program for UW-Madison Department of Curriculum and Instruction.

The authors want to acknowledge the work of the National Women's Health Network's Hormone Education Campaign in providing the key leadership for US women in the evaluation and critique of menopausal hormones. The excellent publications and testimonies before Food and Drug Administration Committees have been extremely valuable in preparing this paper. *Taking Hormones and Women's Health* is available for $5 (+ postage) from the National Women's Health Network, 1325 G Street, N.W., Washington DC, 20005 USA.

Women's Health, 52 Featherstone Street, London, EC1Y 8RT.

References

APPEL, Lawrence, J. and BUSH, Trudy (1991) 'Preventing Heart Disease in Women. Another Role for Aspirin' *Journal of the American Medical Association* Vol. 266, pp. 565–6.

BERGKVIST, Leif et al. (1989) 'The Risk of Breast Cancer after Estrogen and Estrogen-progestin Replacement' *The New England Journal of Medicine* Vol. 321, No. 5, pp. 293–7.

BROWN, Susan (1988) 'Osteoporosis: An Anthropologist Sorts Fact from Fallacy', unpublished longer version of article which was edited and appeared as 'Osteoporosis: Sorting Fact from Fallacy' in (National Women's Health Network) *Network News* July/August, pp. 1, 5–6.

BUSH, Trudy, FRIED, Linda P. and BARRETT-CONNOR, Elizabeth (1988) 'Cholesterol Lipoproteins and Coronary Heart Disease in Women' *Clinical Chemistry* Vol. 34, No. 8(B), pp. B60–B70.

CAULEY, Jane, A. (1988) and GUTAI, James P., KULLER, Lewis H., LEDONNA, Dorothea, SANDLER, Rivka B., SASHIN, Donald and POWELL, John G. (1988) 'Endogenous Estrogen Levels and Calcium Intakes in Postmenopausal Women' *Journal of the American Medical Association* Vol. 260, No. 21, pp. 3150–5.

CEDAR RAPIDS GAZETTE (1991) 'Estrogen Cuts Heart Disease Risk: Study' *Cedar Rapids (Iowa) Gazette* September 12.

COLDITZ, G. A. STAMPFER, M. J., WILLETT, W. C. et al. (1990) 'Prospective Study of Estrogen Replacement Therapy and Risk of Breast Cancer in Postmenopausal Women' *Journal of the American Medical Association* Vol. 264, pp. 2648–53.

DEJANIKUS, Tacie (1985) 'Major Drug Manufacturer Funds Osteoporosis Education Campaign' (National Women's Health Network) *Network News* May/June, pp. 1, 3.

EAGEN, Andrea Boroff (1989) 'Hormone Replacement Therapy Overview' (National Women's Health Network) *Network News* May/June, pp. 1,3.

ETTINGER, Bruce (1987) 'Update: Estrogen and Postmenopausal osteoporosis 1976–1986' *Health Values* Vol. 11, No. 4, pp. 31–6.

FINN, Susan (1987) 'Osteoporosis: A Nutritionist's Approach' *Health Values* Vol. 11, No. 4, pp. 20–3.

FUGH-BERMAN, Adrienne (1991) 'Tamoxifen in Healthy Women: Preventative Health or Preventing Health? (National Women's Health Network) *Network News* September/October, pp. 3–4.

GIGES, Nancy (1986) 'Calcium Market Shrugs Off Study' *Advertising Age* Vol. 59, pp. 49,56.

GOODMAN, Carol E. (1987) 'Osteoporosis and Physical Activity' *Health Values* Vol. 11, No. 4, pp. 24–30.

KIRKPATRICK, Mary (1987) 'A Self Care Model for Osteoporosis' *Health Values* Vol. 11, No. 4, pp. 44–50.

KOLATA, Gina (1990) 'Cancer Risk in Estrogen is Slight, Study Asserts' *New York Times* 28 November, p. A11.

—— (1991a) 'Women Don't Get Equal Heart Care' *New York Times* 25 July, pp. A1, A9.

—— (1991b) 'Estrogen After Menopause Cuts Heart Attack Risk, Study Finds' *New York Times* 12 September, pp. A1, A13.

—— (1991c) 'Women Face Dilemma Over Estrogen Therapy' *New York Times* 17 September.

MACPHERSON, Kathleen I. (1987) 'Osteoporosis: The New Flaw in Woman or in Science?' *Health Values* Vol. 11, No. 4, pp. 57–61.

MANSON, J. E., STAMPFER, M. J., COLDITZ, G. A. et al. (1991) 'A Prospective Study of Aspirin Use and Primary Prevention of Cardiovascular Disease in Women' *Journal of the American Medical Association*, Vol. 266, pp. 521–7.

MCDONNELL, Jessop M., LANE, Joseph M., and ZIMMERMAN, Peter A. (1987) 'Osteoporosis: Definition, Risk Factors, Etiology and Diagnosis' *Health Values* Vol. 11, No. 4, pp. 10–15.

MYERS, Ann H., BAKER, Susan P., VANNATTA, Mark L., ABBEY, Helen, and ROBINSON, Elizabeth G. (1991) 'Risk Factors Associated with Falls and Injuries among Elderly Institutionalized Persons' *American Journal of Epidemiology* Vol. 133, No. 11, pp. 1179–90.

NAPOLI, Maryann (1988) 'Screening for Osteoporosis: An Idea Whose Time Has Not Yet Come' in WORCESTER and WHATLEY (1988b) pp. 115–19.

NATIONAL PRESCRIPTIONS AUDIT, IMS America Ltd., prepared for the National Women's Health Network (hormones and breast cancer files) by the USA Food and Drug Administration Staff, February, 1990.

NATIONAL WOMEN'S HEALTH NETWORK (1989) *Taking Hormones and Women's Health* (available from the NWHN, 1325 G Street, N.W., Washington DC 20005, USA).

NOTELOVITZ, Morris and WARE, Marsha (1982) *Stand Tall! The Informed Woman's Guide to Preventing Osteoporosis*. Gainesville, Florida: Triad.

OTT, Susan (1986) 'Should Women Get Screening Bone Mass Measurements?' *Annals of Internal Medicine* Vol. 104, No. 6, pp. 874–6.

PARFITT, M. (1984) 'Definition of Osteoporosis: Age-related Loss of Bone and its Relationship to Increased Fracture Risk', presented at the National Institutes of Health Consensus Development Conference on Osteoporosis, Bethesda, Maryland, 1–2 April, quoted in MACPHERSON (1987).

PARTLOW, Lian (1991) Personal communication.

PEARSON, Cindy (1991) Testimony before the USA Food and Drug Administration

Select Committee on Ageing, Subcommittee on Housing and Consumer Interests, 30 May.

ROVNER, Sandy (1990) 'Estrogen Therapy: More Data, Less Certainty' *Washington Post Health* 4 September p. 9.

SLOANE, Ethel (1985) *Biology of Women* New York: John Wiley.

SOJOURNER (1991) 'Debating Estrogen Replacement Therapy' *Sojourner-The Women's Forum* November, pp. 13–14.

SPECTER, Michael (1989) 'Hormone Use in Menopause Tied to Cancer' *Washington Post* 3 August, p. 1.

STEERING COMMITTEE OF THE PHYSICIANS' HEALTH STUDY GROUP (1989) 'Final Report on the Aspirin Component of the Ongoing Physicians' Health Study' *New England Journal of Medicine* Vol. 321, pp. 129–35.

STEINBERG, Karen, THACKER, Stephen, SMITH, Jay et al. (1991) 'A Meta-analysis of the Effect of Estrogen Replacement Therapy on the Risk of Breast Cancer' *Journal of the American Medical Association* Vol. 265, pp. 1985–90.

WATERHOUSE, Mindy (1990) 'A Time Line: Premarin', National Women's Health Network Fact Sheet, prepared spring.

WHATLEY, Mariamne H. (1988a) 'Screening is Calculated Exploitation' (National Women's Health Network) *Network News* January/February, pp. 1,3.

——— (1988b) 'Women, Exercise and Physical Potential' in WORCESTER and WHATLEY (1988b).

WHATLEY, Mariamne H. and WORCESTER, Nancy (1989) 'The Role of Technology in the Co-optation of the Women's Health Movement: The Case Study of Osteoporosis and Breast Cancer Screening' in RATCLIFF, Kathryn Strother, et al., *Healing Technology – Feminist Perspectives* Ann Arbor, Michigan: University of Michigan Press, pp. 199–220.

WINSLOW, Ron (1991) 'Women Face Treatment Gap in Heart Disease' *Wall Street Journal* July 25, pp. B1, B4.

WOLFE, Sidney M. (1991a) editor, 'Risk Factors for Falls in the Elderly' (Public Citizens Health Research Group) *Health Letter* Vol. 7, No. 8, p. 10.

——— (1991b) 'New Evidence that Menopausal Estrogens Cause Breast Cancer; Further Doubts About Prevention of Heart Disease' (Public Citizens Health Research Group) *Health Letter* June, pp. 4–6.

WORCESTER, Nancy and WHATLEY, Mariamne H. (1988a) 'The Response of the Health Care System to the Women's Health Movement: The Selling of Women's Health Centers' in ROSSER, Sue V. (1988) *Feminism Within the Science and Health Care Professions: Overcoming Resistance*, Oxford: Pergamon Press, pp. 117–30.

WORCESTER, Nancy and WHATLEY, Mariamne H. (1988b) editors, *Women's Health: Readings on Social, Economic and Political Issues* Dubuque, Iowa: Kendall/Hunt.

THE CANCER DRAWINGS OF CATHERINE ARTHUR

Amanda Sebestyen

At the age of forty-eight Catherine Arthur gave up her job as a technical design journalist to go to Hornsey School of Art. Shortly after completing her course she discovered that she had breast cancer. Over the past year Catherine Arthur has composed a unique cycle of drawings, mythologizing the crisis in her body, reinterpreting ancient symbols as well as creating new ones of her own. This article is extended from a speech given at Lauderdale House in London for the opening of the exhibition 'Love and Pain: the cancer drawings and erotic drawings of Catherine Arthur'.

One of the claims that art has made for itself in this century is of seeing and expressing human suffering in a new way – in particular, by being able to look within. Since the women's movement began, that act of looking within has taken the very specific discipline of looking at our own bodies, and working on *them* as a matter of art.

Again, since the women's movement we've also been able to see certain earlier women artists – considered quite minor and merely 'interesting' before – as tremendously important. Artists like Frida Kahlo, seriously disabled through a hideous accident when she was very young, who made art from the iron corset which she was forced to wear, and other images of immense beauty and strength out of events in her body; or the surrealist Meret Oppenheim, who suffered from repeated mental breakdown and was constantly starting again, using *new* materials and *new* vision. It is now not only women/feminists who see these figures as very important. Frida Kahlo and Meret Oppenheim have been, so to speak, welcomed into the body of 'great art'.

Catherine Arthur's drawings come from inside a tradition of highly self-aware and self-conscious women's art which has taken real root in the last twenty years, as do Jo Spence's photographic chronicles of her

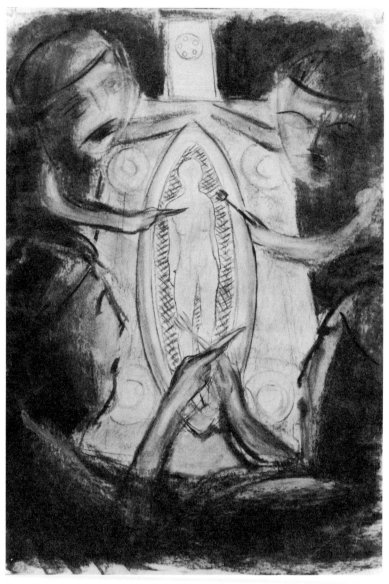

Figure 1. Surgery: The Table.

own cancer experiences. These have crashed the boundaries between conceptual art, documentary, family snapshot, therapy, health re-education/demystification and all-out battle. At first sight, Jo's polemic of outrage, with its scrawled Dada jokes and open commitment to instruction and social change, is at the opposite pole from Catherine Arthur's meditations on life and death. Catherine's drawings work from inside the territory of fine art and classical tradition as well as

Figure 2. Mrs Beeton's Cow.

feminism. Catherine has undergone the orthodox medical treatments for cancer, Jo has opposed them and documented her alternative choice.

But looking closer, I see connexions. Both artists view the medical profession as cannibals, for a start. In Catherine's drawing 'Surgery: The Table' (Fig. 1), the doctors are priestly despots carving up a woman's body in some ancient sacrificial rite. The second Surgery picture, 'Mrs Beeton's Cow' (Fig. 2) shows the woman on all fours, marked out like joints of meat (remember Jo Spence's shot of her breast marked for the knife?). In one of her most inventive drawings Catherine uses a forgotten myth to shed chilling light on a routine medical practice, by the juxtaposition 'Chemotherapy: Sedna' (Fig. 3). Sedna was the daughter of an Inuit god who refused to marry the man her father chose for her. In revenge she was forced to marry her father's dogs, and to escape she flung herself into the sea. As she fell into the water all the different parts of Sedna's body fell apart and became the different animals of the ocean. Catherine used this image because chemotherapy makes the patient feel as if different parts of the body are walking off in different directions.

Of recent women artists one of the most interesting for us is Clare Collison who, before she got ME, used to make the most meticulously posed photographs of herself incorporating hundreds of tiny items. She now has to delegate the stages of making the picture, photographing each object separately and sticking it to the background before putting herself inside. Then the picture goes to a photocopier who can blow it up to life size in nine sheets of A4 paper. The pictures are huge but they're

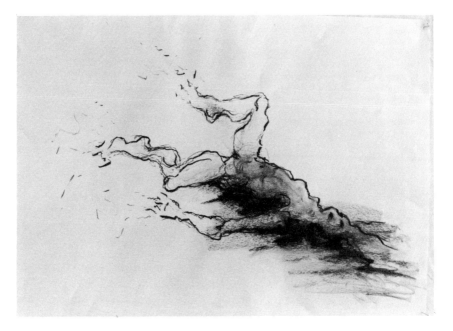

Figure 3. Chemotherapy: Sedna.

now simple (and unpredictable) to make. What interests me in Catherine Arthur's work is that there are so many layers of meaning and yet the technique is simple and portable. The artist has had to adapt the materials to what she can do now.

Within the period of the women's movement, there have been certain men who've been prepared to show the same self-awareness. When I look at the Cancer Drawings I'm also reminded of Rotimi Fani-Kayode, who died last year of meningitis and whose photographs played with the signs of the gay subculture, alternating them with signs of the threat of death and of spiritual renewal. In much the same way, for instance, some of Catherine's pictures use the shaved scalp. When people undergo chemotherapy they lose their hair; here, sometimes the hair is drawn like flames, sometimes like twigs cracking, but sometimes it's seen as dyke fashion while the names of medications are scrawled as graffiti on the wall. There's a play between sexual rebellion and the threat of death.

Donald Rodney is an artist who suffers from sickle cell anaemia, an illness specific to people of African descent. He has carved immense murals out of X-ray plates of his own body, and he's also made art with his own blood circulating along a map of the slave-trade routes.

In Catherine Arthur's Cancer Drawings the image which I find central is embedded in 'Fear' (Fig. 4) – that drawing of the breast as a whirlpool with the growth inside it, like a nipple but also the vortex in which someone is drowning. As her arm reaches out for help it twists in the shape of a shrivelled branch – but right in the middle of the palm there's a little falling figure.

Figure 4. Fear.

This figure is something I've only ever seen shown before as male. Usually it's Prometheus, who brings art and science to human beings by rebelling against the gods, or Phaeton who flies too near the sun and gets burned; or maybe Milton's Satan – or Blake's Satan, who was Blake's hero. But always this male person, male artist. When you see the figure for the first time as female, it becomes quite different. Suddenly, in place of an everlasting fall, you see a baby being born. The

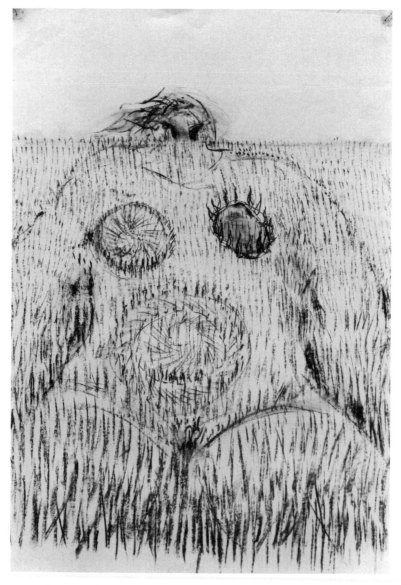

Figure 5. Corn Circles.

same figure comes into one of Catherine's erotic drawings. Bright red, upside down beside a group of women making love, it becomes an emblem of ecstasy and rebirth.

Sometimes Catherine's cancer is seen as growth – a foetus, an egg, a blazing coal, or a moon glowing radioactively in the bosom of a night-time goddess. More often there's the many sided image of a hole – it's the round stigma in the centre of a hand, it's the break in the sky

Figure 6. Standing Stones.

caused by the same radiation which causes and is used to cure cancer, it's the opening of birth through which the woman with cancer falls. In the extraordinary 'Corn Circles' (Fig. 5), where a female body is seen as an earthwork furred over with grass, the circle over one breast is a scorched hole too. In 'Surgery' the dish on which the doctors carve a woman is the shape of another opening, both a vagina and a scar.

When Meret Oppenheim returned to the art world after a gap of more than twenty years she too presented us with the spectacle of a woman being carved up and eaten – she served a 'Love Feast' on a woman's body and made the guests eat. Something Catherine Arthur shares with Meret Oppenheim is an occasionally quite biting wit. I notice a playing with images which are extremely painful but at the same time funny. Catherine uses the image of the lopped-off breast in relation to the Amazons, where it's always supposed to be an option for female power, not a mutilation. In 'Standing Stones' (Fig. 6) there's a side reference to the tradition of the modernist nude sculpture, which makes the female body itself into a kind of standing stone with a hole where the breast is meant to be. In 'Wise Night' (Fig. 7), the goddess looms over an unmistakable North London house and small middle-class car.

What is very moving is the way that sarcasm comes together with speculation on life and death, or even of death as the entrance to a new kind of life. Because of this astringent way of juxtaposing images, the consolations and terrors of different religions can be explored without being pious. Siting a strange nativity scene in the black cave of an

Figure 7. Wise Night.

Amerindian goddess, the artist can see herself bandaged and sucking, like a baby and a corpse at once. The Christian myth of 'The Pelican's Breast' (Fig. 8), like the more usual feminist consolatory myth of the Amazon, makes losing the breast a sacrificial choice. Some choice.

Catherine Arthur's irony informs her most beautiful image of death, 'Boudicca' (Fig. 9). A tree carries life forward, fed by the body of a

Figure 8. The Pelican's Breast.

woman. At the same time the tree is a placenta, nourishing her as a
foetus waiting under the earth. The lost breast, inside the skeleton,
flowers as a rose. But the tree is exactly the shape of a mushroom cloud.
And, incidentally, Boadicea is supposed to have been buried on
Parliament Hill, around the corner from that North London house
where the Cancer Drawings are made.

Figure 9. Boudicca.

Notes

Amanda Sebestyen is a freelance journalist and editor. She was an art critic for *City Limits* and the *New Statesman*, edited her own magazine, *SPLIT*, and has recently worked on *Catalyst* and *Casa Blanca*. She has edited several books including *68–78–88 – Women's Liberation to Feminism*, for Prism Press.

Catherine Arthur died at home on 1 December 1991. Catherine was born in Toronto, Canada, in 1937. She came to London in the early 1960s and worked as a technical journalist specializing in printing, type and design. In 1985 she took up full-time study at Hornsey School of Art. She developed cancer shortly after completing her course. Throughout her illness and treatment (surgery, radiotherapy, chemotherapy) she continued to work at her art, producing drawings, colour drawings and cartoons.

TEN YEARS OF WOMEN'S HEALTH: 1982–92

Barbara James

In 1992, Women's Health, a London-based resource centre, is celebrating its tenth anniversary. This is the first in a series of interviews, articles and other collections of information through which the organization will look back over its history. The results of these examinations will be produced as articles in the anniversary newsletter, or stored in Women's Health's archives for the use of workers in the centre, historians and those who use the centre.

Women's Health formed from the merger in 1988 of two organizations, Women's Reproductive Rights Information Centre (WRRIC) and Women's Health Information Centre (WHIC). WHIC was established with its first funding in 1982 and WRRIC followed after a split within the National Abortion Campaign in 1983. At the time of the merger the new organization called itself the Women's Health and Reproductive Rights Information Centre (WHRRIC), a name chosen to ensure that the dual origins were reflected. The final (we hope!) name change is a result of a number of factors including an increased sense of identity and cohesion within the organization and a desire for a more concise name that still reflects the work of the centre.

The organization has existed over a period of time which has been notable for its constancy and its change. The battle for abortion rights has been ongoing, both in specific campaigns, such as the Alton bill and in less visible but continuing conditions, such as the general erosion of provision of abortion. Cervical and breast cancer continue to be major causes of death despite attempts to improve the screening programme. But new technology, in the field of reproductive technology and elsewhere, has been established as a norm in a way scarcely imagined a decade ago. Single women and lesbians are having children despite the interference of the state and media. Hormone replacement therapy has become one of the most hotly debated treatment regimes. HIV and AIDS are having an overwhelming effect on women's health and reproductive issues. The 'contract culture' is under way. Women's Health has had to respond to these and numerous other concerns and challenges with ever-decreasing financial security.

One of the major internal events of the past decade was the merger of the two organizations. Although there was some initial reluctance, the merger was in fact a natural one, given that the organizations were both information centres in fields whose concerns are so interdependent. Women's health and reproductive issues are impossible to divide – how can infertility as a reproductive rights issue be separated from the health issue of endometriosis, a frequent cause of infertility? But initially the merger was required by funders rather than motivated by the organizations themselves and considerable early resistance had to be overcome. The cost in disruption was immeasurable; it is the 'chaos' referred to in the discussion below. However, the merger has also allowed those who work in the centre to stand back and develop a clearer set of goals from which to work and to develop a wider and more cohesive base for analysing the ever-increasing range of issues facing the women's health movement today.

Unfortunately, the potentially increased strength of the organization has been somewhat undermined by financial insecurity since the merger. Women's Health is not alone – thousands of voluntary organizations are looking to overstretched funders for a limited amount of money. Each new project undertaken by the centre must be considered in terms of its financial potentials, and those that are not self-supporting must be balanced off against those that are. In addition, the increased demands as a result of the closures of hundreds of voluntary organizations across Britain, the changes in the NHS and the ever-increasing numbers of health issues for consideration result in a heavy load for the centre's workers.

The range of services provided by the centre is broad and there is considerable flexibility in the development of new projects. The core tasks of the centre are integrated to provide information on health and reproductive issues to as many users as possible. The resource centre has the largest collection of materials devoted specifically to women's health issues in the country. The collection includes books, leaflets, journals and articles from perspectives ranging from feminist to sociological, to traditional and complementary medical therapies. The complex classification system, developed by Lisa Saffron especially on women's health's topics, is computerized and allows quick access to the materials. We refer enquirers using our database to support groups, individuals, organizations and government agencies all over the country. Our enquiry service answers questions from individuals, the media, health professionals and others. Outreach work concentrates on women who are least likely to have good access to health information – older women, women whose first language is not English, black women, low-income women. Our publications list includes almost 50 titles.

Lisa Saffron.

Special projects with other organizations have ranged from the translation of a set of leaflets into Urdu, to a national conference for health professionals on cervical smears and setting up a network for those affected by diethylstilboestrol.

The centre has provided an opportunity to develop new ways of working. In a time when many voluntary organizations which started off as collectives are opting for directors and hierarchical structures, Women's Health has maintained the collective process – to the extent that it is possible for *any* organization to work nonhierarchically. The length of time in the organization, ethnicity, job done, sexual orientation, ability to speak up in meetings and numerous other factors have all worked in a number of different ways to influence and interfere with collective working. Despite the frustration with collective working expressed in the interview, the general feeling of the workers who remain is that, in spite of its many drawbacks, the collective processes established within the organization meet their needs to a greater extent than other systems.

When it is possible to rise above the stresses of everyday work, it is with pride and even excitement that the workers look at the accomplishments of the centre. We have been in a position to influence the field of women's health and reproductive rights, to provide information and support to women who need it and who, in many cases would not receive it otherwise. We are lucky to work in a field we really care about and feel committed to. We even have fun doing it.

I organized a discussion with Lisa Saffron and Marge Berer, two of the original workers involved in the establishment of the two centres. Both have gone on to other work. Marge went to work for the Women's Global Network for Reproductive Rights. Now she is working on a resource book on women, HIV and AIDS and other reproductive health publications. Lisa is employed by an environmental-health project and is working on the second edition of her book, *Getting Pregnant Our Own Way: A Woman's Guide to Self-insemination*.

Origins of the organizations

Lisa: There was a group of women who formed out of the Politics of Health Group, which had been meeting in the late seventies – a mixed organization. They had general meetings every so often and various groups developed out of those forums, like the politics of food group. The women's health group had a goal of setting up a women's health information centre. They met together and applied for funds for several years before they got a grant from the Equal Opportunities Commission, of about £7,000. They'd been talking in general terms for several years; they didn't really have a clear concept of what they wanted, other than an information centre. There were several GPs and medical students, health-education workers and medical sociologists. They were all involved in health and they all identified themselves as socialists.

There were various problems that came up at every stage. And I think in the early stages the problems were that the needs of the collective – which at that point was the management committee – were different from the needs of the paid worker. We went together on various weekends to talk about the problems. What emerged was that the management committee really needed a support group for themselves as health professionals. They were quite clear about it. I needed management and practical help with setting up a completely new centre from scratch – totally from scratch, without even an office. More importantly, I didn't have a clear concept of what we were setting up. It was difficult to have discussions that met everyone's needs. There were a lot of hurt feelings and tensions in these meetings because of that. Also, the voluntary management committee were all working full time in demanding jobs and they did not have the time. They were very committed and they had vision, but they didn't have the time to deal with the nitty-gritty and I did feel quite isolated. I was on my own for the first year and a half. Before the office was found I was at home with boxes of files stored in my bedroom!

There were the practical realities, like being in an isolated office in a community centre no one ever went to, but I think there was also the problem that they thought that now we have money, the money will do everything we want done.

Marge Berer.

Marge: I was employed by the National Abortion Campaign (NAC). When I started there in 1980, it was a mass political campaign, and then suddenly it wasn't mass anymore. We ended up twirling round in circles, trying to decide what it was going to be instead. Mass movements around abortion died all over Europe around the end of the seventies. Practically every European country had at least decriminalized abortion, and the abortion rights movements felt that they had achieved their goals. The mass of women thought, 'Well, we've done that one' and went home. We had arguments in the early 1980s about whether NAC should be primarily about abortion or expand into reproductive rights more broadly, at a point when the organization possibly wasn't going to be about anything at all anymore. There was a major battle that led to a split at the NAC national conference in 1983. I don't think a year has gone by since then that I haven't asked myself if it was a major mistake for that split to have occurred, and what could have been done to avoid it, if anything. It had real consequences for the functioning of NAC, because afterwards the bulk of its support was lost except for a core of dedicated women and it was pretty well deserted by the socialist left who had fought to keep it an abortion campaign to begin with.

We set up WRRIC in late 1983, at a time when the concept of reproductive rights was new. WHIC developed out of the needs of professional women needing a space to talk and then wanting to provide information to other people, whereas WRRIC developed out of a political campaign. Because the political side of things was dying down, information was seen to be a necessity. We weren't coming from the same circles. The same thing happened on the international level as well. It seems to me that there's a conflict in that situation between a campaigning organization and an information and service-providing organization.

In this country feminists didn't consider providing women's health services, because that was the job of the NHS. But the conflict between doing political work and doing information work, as if the two things were different (which I don't think they are) leads to these different phases of the organizations. So WRRIC ended up mainly as an information centre, which I personally found extremely disappointing, although I understand it now. A reproductive rights *campaign*, which in a sense is what we thought we were fighting to have, never really got off the ground or defined itself. In the end, the two separate information centres, after a great deal of resistance all around, got themselves together to become one thing. Or rather, were forced to get together. Although you and I did have talks about it fairly early on.

The merger

Barbara: I remember WHIC members bringing up merger proposals a number of times, but it was a very difficult issue.
Lisa: It became a territorial issue.
Marge:We were worried about losing our identity if we merged. It was the information versus the reproductive rights approach, as well.
Barbara: Another point is that any merger like that, at least the ones that are imposed from outside, tend to be seen by those who impose them as a chance to save money, to eliminate 'duplication'. Financially speaking, the merger of WHIC and WRRIC was a cut, and a major one. So a merger is a threatening thing in that way.
Lisa: But from the point of view of the politics of what we were doing, there was always some confusion about why there was a separation between the two organizations.
Marge: That's partly because WRRIC became something similar to WHIC when in fact that wasn't our original intention. However, it was difficult to let go of that concept even when it had not been put into practice.

Information provision as political action

Lisa: The issue of Depo Provera came up very early in the first year and a half. One member of the WHIC collective fought very hard for WHIC to be involved. Her vision was that WHIC would be a campaigning body, lobbying Parliament on this type of issue. There was a lot of resistance from the rest of the collective who felt that it was too early in our development for that kind of involvement and that was true at some levels. They wanted us to deliberate on what we were setting up. They didn't want to simply launch into action. It's also true that some of the collective might have felt uncomfortable with the concept of a politically active, lobbying centre.

Marge: I worked non-stop on that Depo Provera document for five months. I also wanted NAC and then WRRIC to take on that kind of work.

Lisa: Organizationally, it was very difficult. We were still at the stage of wondering what it was we were setting up, which photocopier to get, and the practicalities of finding an office. All of a sudden the Depo Provera issue came up, and we plunged into it; after the dispute among the collective, one member essentially forced the rest to work on it.

Barbara: Somehow I have been able to feel that I am getting done what I want to do within the collective structure – or if not what I want to do, since I am not particularly fond of fundraising – what the centre needs to do. Of course, that is within the constraints which we are now operating under. We have managed to do a lot of useful work, not necessarily direct political lobbying, but we have had considerable influence in a number of areas. We have made submissions to the House of Commons Select Committee on AIDS, we are contacted regularly by the media on all areas of women's health and reproductive issues, we work with the Department of Health on HIV and AIDS, we have produced a television programme on infertility and reproductive technology.

However, we are restricted in how we are able to express ourselves. We have had a funder tell us that we were putting our funding at risk by using the phrase 'the Thatcher government' instead of the more respectful 'Mrs Thatcher's government'. So if we are being criticized for using what I would have thought was a pretty standard phrase, what kind of hard-hitting political lobbying could we do?

Marge: That's a consequence of having taken on charitable status to get money.

Barbara: Certainly, but if an organization wants to function on the scale we do, seeking funding is unavoidable. That's why I think lobbying is more the responsibility of someone like you or independent groups not under our constraints.

Marge: Yes, but that's not possible for individuals or in a vacuum.

Lisa: Perhaps that issue has been the cause of some of the confusion about the role of the centre, since most of the women who started both WHIC and WRRIC and who have worked in the centres have been politically motivated, in whatever way you define that. Because we have gone for the position of accepting money which constrains what we can do, it is difficult to see the difference between us and other information services.

Marge: I don't like the idea that giving information is not political.

Lisa: That's not what I meant. The whole women's health movement is giving information and it's not all political, by any means. Just because you give information doesn't mean you're political.

Marge: But it also doesn't mean that you're not. We have lost track of the word feminist in all of this. We've lost the idea of *why* you give women information, *how* you give women information and *what* you're giving it to them for.

Lisa: In the early years especially there was a lot of confusion. In the last year I worked at WHRRIC, we attempted a definition of our goals, and some of what you're talking about came up, do you remember?

Barbara: We did come up with a useful set of goals. Many organizations still haven't established their goals after years of work! Our goals actually mean something. So much so that I have had funders suggest we are putting people off by using the 'f' word too often. 'Feminist', I mean!

Marge: I'm not sure what feminism means, anyway. There are women running around who are anti-abortion, anti-reproductive technology, as well as those who are for abortion and who figure that quite a bit of reproductive technology is a very good thing for women and they all call themselves feminist. What do the words women's health mean?

Barbara: What, you want us to change our name again?

Lisa: It's important to get back to goals – it would have been good if we had been able to have those goal-setting sessions earlier in our history.

Marge: We didn't have them in WRRIC, either, because whenever we started we found that we didn't necessarily agree, and then what were we going to do about our disagreement as a collective? It's one of the

---

Aims

- To empower women to make their own informed decisions about the health and reproductive choices they face
- To inform women of their reproductive rights and to provide information about women's health issues
- To provide a quality service in a feminist and women-centred framework
- To develop and promote a feminist perspective of women's health and reproductive rights, which arises out of women's experiences rather than from the state or the medical profession
- To focus on those women's health issues such as cervical cancer, menstrual problems, infertility, etc., which are not adequately covered by existing groups
- To support self-help and the sharing of experiences among women and to validate women's own experiences

saddest and most amazing parts of this – if you don't fix your goals clearly enough, anyone who thinks that they support women's health or women's reproductive rights, belongs in that centre. But they may have widely diverging goals. If you're a collective, you're not allowed to acknowledge those differences and it is one of the causes of great conflict. It often means that you don't know how to solve the conflicts. Whose vision is chosen to follow?

Barbara: The chaos of the merger of WHIC and WRRIC did bring about a few useful things. For example, the set of goals we formulated is still useful. They're essential for new workers to understand what the organization stands for. We have reasons for the various jobs we do, and we can use that set of goals to evaluate the work we do. Although the first goal has to be 'to make money'. That is now the aim we have to base everything else that we do on, but that's another story.

Lisa: Everyone's in that position, no matter what world you're in.

Marge: In those early years, both organizations had to go through a process before reaching the point of being able to make concrete statements of aim.

Lisa: What could have been different, or was it just not possible?

Marge: Let's get back to the point about giving information as political action. Giving information to an individual woman to empower her to handle a doctor, to take control of her own health care, to help her to feel OK about something that went wrong that nobody else gave her support through: that's all personal/political. Whereas going down to Parliament and lobbying when there's a bill you think shouldn't go through is doing politics at a national level, at a collective level, a mass level, a policy level. It's not simply for the individual. You can get lost in helping individuals by ignoring the policy. Or being forced to ignore the policies – that's more what is going on at this stage. Groups like Women's Health are not being permitted to take any steps to influence the policy because it would mean coming down on one side or the other, or you were taking a position against the government and the government is giving you money.

Barbara: There are situations where various government departments or committees ask us to make submissions or provide information. Perhaps as important is the media work we do, although it is some of our most difficult work, trying to ensure journalists get it right. With recent issues like the virgin birth, we had a major opportunity to promote a pro-choice position all over the country in all the media. That isn't lobbying in the strict sense.

Marge: But it's certainly political work.

Barbara: One of the most significant changes in what we were allowed to talk about came with Clause 28. Government equal opportunities monitoring forms used to ask about the sexual orientation of staff and users, but that was dropped as soon as the clause went through. But it's not simply lack of concern about whether we are meeting the needs of lesbians. We now have a clause in the contract with our main funding body which states that our continued funding is dependent upon *not*

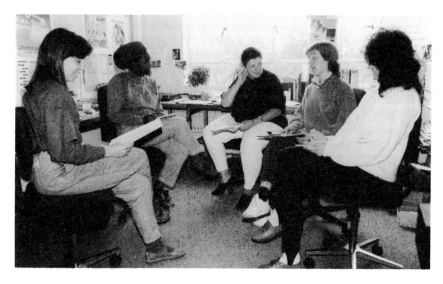

WRRIC workers, 1987.

promoting homosexuality. We used to carry the book written by Lisa, *Getting Pregnant Our Own Way; A Woman's Guide to Self-insemination*, which was incredibly popular with both lesbians and single heterosexual women who wanted to get pregnant. We were told specifically to stop selling that book. We are completely vulnerable to this kind of legislation, since we rely so heavily on government funding. Fortunately, that book is going to be brought out by a publisher but it leaves us in a position of having to figure out how to serve and support the same constituency of women.

Changes in the NHS bring up more difficulties. We aren't able to do the analysis we want to in our publications. Because we are not commenting directly on the health service, we can end up appearing more conservative than organizations like the British Medical Association which condemns changes in the NHS.

Marge: That's a difference from when I worked at WRRIC. It wasn't an issue. I call all of that political work and that's the part I like to do the best.

Lisa: But we have always had other work areas to concentrate on as well. One of the major time consumers has always been answering enquiries, which was one of the earliest services started in both WHIC and WRRIC. Once an organization establishes a phone answering service for individuals, it takes on a life of its own. It dominates, because if you're going to run that service, you have to do it properly. It takes up an incredible amount of time. I remember in the early days, trying to be practical about what we could manage, we decided we'd have it open only Tuesday and Thursday.

Barbara: Our funders required that the emphasis be put on the phone

line. They fund you for direct contact with the public. They are primarily interested in outreach and educational work, so we do a lot of that.
Marge: Because they think that's not political.
Barbara: I think most of the organizations that fund us consider what we do political work, in the sense that a more conscious woman is one who has more power over her own health. But certainly their main concern tends to be educational and benevolent. Unfortunately, it's more difficult to get money for the jobs that are necessary to produce leaflets, which we want to do to ensure we reach those who don't contact us directly with an enquiry.
Lisa: That's a bit shortsighted, because Women's Health could be more of a national service. London funders tend not to acknowledge that London, the major city in Britain, has a responsibility to the rest of the country. We could reach so many more women through a greater emphasis on writing, media work, etc. if we didn't concentrate so much on a one-to-one phone service.
Marge: They're not generally interested in the larger picture. They're interested in welfare issues rather than political ones. From their point of view it makes sense to provide a welfare service which deals with individuals who have problems.
Barbara: In the early days there was a very strong sense within the organization that writing leaflets wasn't as important as the phone work. As a matter of fact, nothing was as important as the phone work. Fortunately, the thinking about that has improved, and for several reasons. We have recognized that with limited staffing levels we cannot answer all the questions that callers might have, even if we wanted to. Also we have seen that we can distribute tens of thousands of leaflets all over the country with ease – and women will read them. One of the main factors in this change of emphasis, as usual, has been financial. However much we may want to distribute our information free, we have to make a significant portion of our income from sales – and now we do. We've had to have discussions about accepting publications orders from particular bodies – like drug companies! But we have always determined the circumstances under which leaflets are to be distributed, we have made no changes in the text of the materials we send them and we do not promote any drugs or products, so we feel satisfied.
Marge: What I find very political about giving information is the wider discussion about *what* information you give. What do you say to women who phone up asking about Depo Provera, who've heard it's dangerous but their doctor wants them to have it?
Lisa: Or any issue.
Marge: Yes, but let's take that one since it was so controversial for so long. How do you decide what information is going to be given out about a topic like Depo Provera. If the phone line is going to be such an important part of the work of the centre, the answer to a question like that has to be consistent, no matter who is answering the phone. You can't have one worker saying, 'Yes, it's dangerous, you shouldn't use it'

and another saying 'No it isn't dangerous, but there are these advantages and disadvantages'.

Barbara: No one on a phone line now would categorically tell a woman not to follow a course of treatment. We have tried to be consistent about presenting a well-balanced view about things. In the case of controversial topics like Depo Provera, the woman has often been told the case *for* the treatment, and is calling us to hear about what the problems might be. Through our various processes, like the editor reading new materials for the newsletter, the library worker collecting materials for the resource centre, and the workers doing self-education, we try to develop a balanced viewpoint.

Lisa: There's always difficulty about having a line on particular issues. It's very difficult when you're on the phone with a person. You can't really have 'a line' when you're talking about their decision about what to do . . .

Marge: Oh, but you certainly can have a line.

Barbara: Some people say 'Abortion is murder' or 'HRT will answer all your prayers' or 'No hysterectomies'.

Marge: And others say 'No hormones'. Those are lines.

Lisa: Well, of course, but I don't feel comfortable with that kind of thing. The facts are always so much more messy. A line isn't appropriate.

Marge: I tend to agree with you now, but there are a lot of people who don't.

Lisa: It's simpler to have a line.

Barbara: I think the way Women's Health has evolved can be illustrated by looking at HRT: it took a long time to develop the position, but we give both sides of the picture.

Lisa: That's what I think is good about the materials Women's Health produces. I don't think it's always been achieved, but in general, we've tried to give a range of detailed information to help women make up their own minds. But it's not unproblematic, is it?

Marge: No it isn't because you can still stress certain aspects – benefits as opposed to risks. You can use a language to describe them in such a way that you make a benefit sound negligible, or unimportant, and make a risk sound more risky than it actually is. God knows if it actually is or it isn't – the scientists probably aren't sure.

Lisa: Well, exactly.

Marge: I find these some of the more interesting questions about the kind of work WH does. We had more trouble answering those questions seven or eight years ago than everybody probably does now. It's just as difficult, but then we were more into denying the grey areas.

Lisa: That comes out of a political background, where you're more likely to have slogans.

Barbara: And that's why it took several years to come up with a position on HRT.

Collective working

Lisa: Things have really changed since the beginning of the organization. Initially, at WHIC because I was the only worker, working with a voluntary collective, there was considerable confusion about how to get things done. I hoped for direction which I didn't get. I felt frustrated, the collective felt frustrated.

Marge: There's something about collectives that means that you're not allowed to come up with ideas of your own – *everybody* has to have the idea first, and then you can do it. Even when you have your own idea, you feel there's something wrong with being left to get on with it yourself – it's supposed to be collective. Whereas if you've been hired, handed the job, told from the beginning, 'You're on your own, it's up to you, we want this centre, we want it to be like this – good luck. You can phone us up for this that and the other thing . . .'

Lisa: But only this that and the other thing . . .

Marge: Then you could have done it or not done it as you chose.

Lisa: You're right that in a collective if you have an idea you just can't take it and go off with it, you have to get approval. Part of it is about accountability. That's what is behind it. It's not a bad thing in itself, but it doesn't seem a very effective way to work.

Barbara: Also for you another thing was that this was an original start, there weren't any other centres like it, you were isolated, you were one worker, alone. As much as anything else the total isolation and the size of the task before you would make the process overwhelming. It was 1982. There was no library, no classification scheme, very little money, and all the services – publications, phone line, outreach, education – were yet to be developed. A less than effective collective process can hardly be blamed for that. A whole new way of working was being evolved at that time. Surely that in itself is a difficult process!

Marge: Another thing was that it was happening just at the point where women's group work was changing from being almost always voluntary to being almost completely paid work. We were dealing with parameters that we knew almost nothing about. We were dealing with people who were getting together for political reasons who were then trying to set up professional or semiprofessional services and information organizations which is quite a major jump.

Lisa: When we started there was a voluntary group of about fourteen women and one worker – me. The concept of collective was different. The conflict was between paid workers and unpaid volunteers not located in the workplace or the sharing of the work. Gradually we moved to being a paid collective of eight as it is now with an unpaid, less visible management group. But at the beginning there were few models of how to work collectively.

Marge: Or of how to set up a feminist organization either. Let alone how to hire a person to work in a collective working situation. There was very little experience. It's been trial and error and struggle, but not chaos.

Lisa: There was a series of meetings of the women's collectives that

WHIC workers, 1987.

were developing at the time. That was very useful. It seemed everyone was having the same problems.

Barbara: What I find rewarding about all this is that throughout the whole difficult process, so much has been accomplished.

Marge: Unbelievable!

Lisa: What amazes me is to think of the quality of service that Women's Health has been giving over the last few years, compared to any other service that you would get – the leaflets on so many topics, the outreach service, the enquiry service, the support . . .

Barbara: Value for money! Well perhaps if we had the funds for it we could institute performance-related pay!

Marge: We did a lot, and we've done a lot right along.

Lisa: I wish I'd felt better about it at the time. There were a lot of frustrations for me. We were trying to redress all the wrongs of society in our little organization. Everything – challenging all power imbalances, changing working conditions, developing new ways of working. But we didn't have the resources to train people, to cover the workload. Once we had a psychotherapist come in to facilitate a meeting. I thought she made one good point: we were taking on too much. We wanted to make everyone happy. We felt distressed by the pain of the women who called.

We didn't have any limits to what we were doing, any realistic limits. Now, I think it's getting to the point where we're more realistic.

Marge: Considering that I haven't worked there for six years, and that I've stayed in the field, when I visit, I am extremely pleased that the resource centre is there for me to take advantage of. It makes me feel very good, walking in, knowing that I had something to do with starting it. And I can remember laughing and having a good time, and working like hell and loving it a lot of the time.

Lisa: Having left and tried to enter a different field, I don't look back and think those were wasted years in any way. I'm very pleased with the service the centre is running. I felt a friendship with the people I worked with, or a friendliness. That's nothing to sneeze at – I don't have it where I work anymore. I also feel good about how WH has progressed with computers, which I resisted madly at first.

Marge: Yeah, I remember when we used to run up and down the building talking about women's politics; now all we do is run up and down the building talking about how to make the computer work.

Lisa: They do take over, don't they, and yet what a difference they have made – the database, the desk-top publishing.

Barbara: Remember those WRRIC leaflets – UG-LY!

Marge: How dare you! I put my blood into those leaflets.

Lisa: The words may have been wonderful . . . but, we've come a long way since then.

Notes

Barbara James was first involved in reproductive rights issues in Canada in 1979. Since 1985 she has worked both at Women's Health and the British Library, which has been a study in contrasts!
Women's Health, 52 Featherstone Street, London EC1Y 8RT

AIDS ACTIVISM

WOMEN AND AIDS ACTIVISM IN VICTORIA, AUSTRALIA

Anne Mitchell

AIDS activism in Australia has been largely left to the men. It is important to remember that our experience of the epidemic has been a unique one in which the devastation in the gay community over the past ten years has not been followed by the expected uncontrolled swell into the IV drug-using community or among large numbers of heterosexuals. Forewarned to some extent and so forearmed, the government and community groups have been able to implement strategies such as widespread needle and syringe exchange programmes which are holding it in uneasy containment. The end result of this is that the number of women infected with HIV is relatively small (81 in Victoria until June 1991 as opposed to 2,589 men). While this obviously means these women experience marginalization and feel the lack of appropriate services, they are also a group rightly fearful for their privacy and an inevitable backlash against themselves and their children. Personal activism or energetic attempts to excite the ire of feminist advocates to act on their behalf can therefore be seen as threatening and out of the question.

The conflict around these issues was nicely illustrated recently in an altercation which ensued between the Positive Women's Support Groups in New South Wales (NSW) and Victoria over the logo adopted by each group. In NSW there are larger numbers of infected women (394 to June 1991) and a stronger history of radical women's activism both in advocacy for infected women and for gender-specific prevention education. The NSW Positive Women's Group adopted as its logo a circle developed out of the women's symbol made up of female figures linked

P SITIVE WOMEN

A support group run by
Women with HIV/AIDS for
Women with HIV/AIDS

We offer -
• one-to-one contact, telephone
  contact &/or regular group
  meetings
• sharing of information
• friendship
• non-judgemental support for
  all Women who are antibody
  positive or have AIDS

Contact -
Positive Women
PO Box 1546
Collingwood 3066
or phone
Gayle Olsen 602 3002
Dawn Gould 417 1759

by hands. This symbol of strength and power contrasted markedly with the pink rose symbol adopted by the Victorian group and denigrated by their NSW sisters as 'looking like a tampon ad'. The Victorian women in their defence argue that their group is a support group to meet emotional and practical needs of members and only an advocacy group in a secondary sense. Many of the women they wish to attract do not recognize the women's symbol or, if they do, do not identify with it. The rose is seen as a rallying point which is feminine and powerful in its capacity to establish a separate identity for women in the male-dominated, sometimes misogynist world of AIDS.

The small numbers of infected women contribute to the lack of feminist activism around AIDS in one final way. Women's health services, in Victoria at least, are notoriously underfunded and neglected. Health issues specific to women are under-researched and poorly prioritized. With large numbers of women still dying of cervical cancer (about 400 a year nationally) for want of a sensitive, accessible nonracist health-care system in which pap smears are routine, the needs of HIV-infected women are somewhat lower on the list for urgent redress. Feminist advocates in the area of women's health in Australia are far more focused on confronting the social inequalities which make women sick in the first place rather than addressing the needs of those with specific illnesses.

This is not to say women with HIV do not gain from the inroads made in this way. Women do, of course, also benefit from the gains made by the articulate and politically skilled middle-class male homosexuals in the community-based AIDS councils and predictably join them in large numbers as volunteer members and support people. Women benefit too from the radical activities of ACT UP, for example around drug trials and treatment issues, and participate and organize protest activities to this end. Nevertheless, they are understandably reluctant to be used as test cases to force medical services reluctantly to accommodate them as the men did earlier in the epidemic, and progress for women will be slow.

In all this there is a further strand of concern for women which it is easy to overlook and that is the potential for social attitudes to infected women to further fuel cherished traditional prejudices against particular groups of women. Just as the upsurge of violence against homosexuals in Australia has arisen out of righteous anger about AIDS and enjoyed a degree of social tolerance, women too have the potential to experience a backlash which is seen as at least 'understandable' where AIDS is involved.

There is considerable debate in Australia about the nature of the responsibility governments have to ensure public health. Much of the community is supporting punitive and restrictive action against those who are infected while advocacy groups are arguing in defence of individual rights. In both NSW and Victoria this debate has come to a head in the media over cases of individual sex workers.

Australian society from its convict origins has been more rigorously grounded in the madonna/whore dichotomy than most. Female sex workers designated 'damned whores' from the pulpits of our past have acted endlessly as scapegoats for a myriad of social problems and moral injustices. If anyone was 'knowingly and recklessly' spreading HIV in the community it was bound to be the damned whores with their traditional fecklessness and their even more terrifying capacity to reach

POSITIVE WOMEN

Individual and Group Support
for and by HIV/AIDS Positive Women

Non-judgemental and completely confidential

For more information, please call
The Women's HIV Support Officer, AIDS Council of NSW, (02) 283 3222,
TTY 283 2088, PO Box 350 Darlinghurst NSW 2010, or
The Counselling Service, Albion Street (AIDS) Centre, (02) 332 1090

Regular evening meetings

the good women and their children through their hapless married male clients. Punitive action was clearly required if the social fabric was to be maintained.

In March 1991, a transsexual sex worker was arrested in Victoria and charged by the police with 'conduct endangering life' and 'conduct likely to cause serious injury'. The Health Department in the state in fact had already quite draconian powers to detain and isolate people who so threatened public health but, committed to a policy of harm minimization and community development in the area, had established a five-step plan of counselling, education and support to precede and possibly avert any need to detain and punish. Following the somewhat maverick police charge, massive media support got behind society's right to be free of this menace to hearth and home, and applauded police action in the face of 'pussy-footing' health authorities. My God, this was not just poofters and junkies – real people could be infected here, this was getting serious!

The human rights issues were taken up here by an unlikely alliance, but one much strengthened by shared oppression. Sex workers in Victoria are very ably supported and defended by the community-based Prostitutes' Collective of Victoria (PCV). While male prostitutes are accommodated in their charter their clientele is predominantly female and their activities are based on sound feminist ideals, many of which seek not simply to advocate for women as less powerful social operators but to actively address the image of the female sex worker as a social enemy. 'No bad women, just bad laws' has been a long time slogan of theirs.

Although the sex worker in question in this case continued to maintain that she had only safe sex, the debate about the criminal nature of her activities shifted to the right of any infected individual to have sex with anyone else. It appeared that Victoria might host a world first here – a court case leading to a legal ruling on the efficacy of safe sex.

At this point PCV combined with ACT UP to defend this most basic of human rights. Following a march under banners reading 'Implement the five-point plan' and 'Sex workers have safe sex, do you?' sex workers, gay men and other interested persons rolled themselves up into sleeping bags on the Arts Centre lawns and simulated various sexual activities. While a lot of outrage and apprehension was created in passers-by, the media responded with surprising good nature to the colourful and, in a sense, well-beloved presence of the sex workers spewed up from their bordellos in St Kilda to storm this citadel of virtue. While it was not the first time they had combined with the gay community to fight a common enemy, their presence was seen to counteract the boredom of another 'gay protest' and focused the issues much more around the way in which society regards women. An outcome of this protest and the debate around it was a small but significant shift of focus to the need to educate male clients of sex workers and to arraign them to take responsibility for their own safety. This was not an inconsiderable gain, nor was the protocol subsequently worked out between health authorities and the police to handle cases of infected sex workers in the future. This specific case, however, is yet to come to court.

It wasn't, of course, a happy-ever-after ending following one fairly desperate event, but it does perhaps indicate that if we are to look for feminist defenders of our sexual rights so acutely linked to AIDS issues for women, we could do worse than to look to sex workers. Rich with success from reforms newly forced on the sex industry, they know what it is to come from a position of 'nothing to lose' and so have the potential for prodigious gains.

Note

Anne Mitchell works in HIV/AIDS education for the Health Department, Victoria. She lives in Melbourne.

AIDS AND WOMEN: A Swiss Perspective

Notes from articles and letters by Charlotte Friedli

> We state that women don't use protective measures; it probably doesn't suit their nature [*sic*] – they should by all means learn to protect themselves.

> In Italy, two hundred children are affected.
> Mr de Lorenzo, Italy's Health Minister

Of course, the Italian Health Minister is not worried about a woman's point of view, his only concern is to highlight whose fault it is that so many children in Italy are affected by the AIDS virus. At a parliamentary session on women one member commented, 'Our state is male to its marrow'.

In politics, science – in all public positions – men make decisions on behalf of 'mankind'. And what about women? Stupid question. Of course she is included in mankind! After all, now women can be present when scientists and politicians discuss subjects like the menopause, birthing techniques, and the conditions of women soldiers in wartime. 'Naturally', those politicians and scientists decide if, when and where AIDS is a woman's problem.

The men of the Swiss Stop AIDS Campaign don't seem to have any scruples about addressing women; their message is: 'Use the condom for your safety and the safety of your partner' – a message which is more suited to their ideas about men's 'nature'. But with a budget of a few million Swiss francs a year, you can't take such details into account; it only affects over half the population! They must imagine that a woman's first attempt to use a condom would leave her with insurmountable problems. Better to assume women have no problems with AIDS as they are 'naturally' faithful; after all, faithfulness training has been part of

their socialization for centuries. This message of faithfulness as protection against AIDS is visually underlined with a golden wedding ring! For some women who find themselves in the 'safety of marriage', the consequences of this message could be fatal.

Last but not least, our men from the Stop AIDS commission have thought about how women could be useful: be in solidarity with men. Here at least women can feel they are being addressed. They carry out nearly 100 per cent of the work, unpaid or underpaid, in or outside the family.

The experts' methodological secrets and their relevance for women

Let's take a close look at the PR methods and strategies of the Stop AIDS experts.

Aim of the campaign: Reach the whole population.

Method: Sympathetically understand the everyday situations of people and create messages everyone can identify with.

Resulting images and scenarios:

Two men friends meet in a bar. First friend to second friend: 'What a good night, last night.' Second friend: 'What do you mean?' They put their heads together and start talking. Suddenly the second friend raises his head. 'I hope you used a condom?!'

Second scene, second message, same place! First man friend to second man friend: 'I've decided to get married. I've had enough of cruising around. With my own wife, at least I know what I've got.'

Several strategies were used to put across these two messages. Besides billboards and ads on TV, the experts produced a so-called soft-porn video. At least I now know how a woman uses a condom. He lolls about on the bed. With erotic movements, she weaves around him and (hey, presto!), she slides the condom over 'him' – he didn't even feel a thing! (Still, I wonder where I can learn this curvatious dance technique.)

I have tried to imagine these scenes substituting women. The scenes are similar, but quite different. Too bad they are but a figment of female imagination.

Two women friends meet in a café. First friend to second: 'I've met a guy; I tell you he is brilliant.' Then they put their heads together and talk until the second friend raises her head: 'Are you crazy? You should have insisted on it or tell him to go to hell!

The scene about faithfulness I leave to your imagination.

But women's ways of thinking are not being considered by the massive campaign for the Swiss people. A small group called Women and AIDS, working without any money from Swiss AIDS, develops all the information which takes women into account. Stop AIDS refused, and still refuses today, to consult women for their campaign for the population as a whole. The experts will continue to bombard women with messages dreamt up by and for men. These messages do not translate into women's everyday situations. Meanwhile, the number of women infected with HIV through heterosexual sex escalates drastically.

Public authorities don't want to talk about it because then it would be known that 'very normal' women have sexual instincts. It is never mentioned that men play the major role in prostitution: for every 1.5 prostitutes there are 98.5 clients. So who and where are the 300,000 Swiss men who regularly exchange money for sexual favours, if possible without condoms?

Does women-oriented AIDS prevention provoke fear?

Is the subject of 'women and AIDS' not wanted because it questions the role of women in this society? If you discount the physical risk of having sex, the actual situation of women in our society plays a significant part in AIDS infection through a male sexual partner. Traditionally, the woman is expected to be passive and has been trained to look after those around her and not think about her own wishes. Women don't know what it means to have their own space; they share the bedroom with their partner. If there is a spare room, it will be his hobby room or office.

She probably 'forgot' that she has the right to have and express her own wishes and needs, because she learned to get her fulfilment and

happiness through meeting her family's needs. It goes without saying that in this situation his sexual needs come first. Considering all this, women are not supposed to have sexual needs.

If women don't manage to express their wishes and conditions (such as for the use of condoms) this selflessness could be fatal in the age of AIDS. There is no getting away from it: successful AIDS prevention demands a change in existing sex-role behaviour. Women must recognize their own needs and wishes, express them, and put them into action. They must find the courage to say no – and to defend their own demands.

What's needed

It's obvious that men and women need different types of counselling. Both people working with men, and those working with women need extra information and training. As women's problems are often caused by men, women counsellors must be available to talk with women.

Prevention programmes must be changed, and good counselling

made available to counter the difficult psychological situation of women who get infected because of incorrect publicity. Women are told they themselves must engage in risky behaviour to become HIV positive. They turn up saying, 'I have always been faithful to my partner, I never thought I was exposed to the virus. How could I know he had a double life?'

Because women's role is generally to care for men, and men feel they need healthy, sexually attractive women to care for them, often women with HIV or AIDS are abandoned by their partners. HIV-positive women may abandon their partners and isolate themselves, because they feel they have lost their reasons for living. As one HIV-positive woman said in a group, 'I can't offer my partner "normal" sexuality, and I can't give him children.' Conversely, women rarely abandon their partners if the partner has HIV or AIDS. Consequently, there must be a lot more outreach to women who are isolating themselves, or helping their partners with AIDS. Women also need accurate counselling about sexuality, childbirth and abortion. Counsellors have to be trained to respond with facts and empathy to talk with women who say, 'I'm pregnant, the doctor wants me to get an abortion, what can I do?'

HIV AND THE INVISIBILITY OF WOMEN: Is there a need to redefine AIDS?

Emily Scharf and Sue Toole

For the 'public' of Britain, HIV and AIDS have only recently become issues for women, due to the publicity about the increased numbers of women diagnosed with AIDS, plus the initial results of the anonymous testing of pregnant women in antenatal clinics.

But HIV has acted as a spotlight, for over a decade, to expose all the inequalities that exist worldwide, including all the familiar women's issues.

The images of women in relation to HIV (where women are visible at all) have reflected society's stereotypic roles: not being seen as people in their own right, but as carers or partners of others; bad women versus good women, and so on. Therefore, we have medical statistics about women based on 'partners of infected men', mothers of infected children (medically described as 'vectors of vertical transmission'), or sex workers blamed for infecting the heterosexual community, and the 'wives at home' as (passive) victims.

HIV exposes all the inequalities of women's positions in society: poorer; less access to health care for themselves; little support in their roles as carers; in less powerful positions to negotiate relationships, including the sexual ('safer sex'). And we hear discussions by some medical professionals about the 'management' of transmission to children – that is, the management of the *mothers* – through obligatory testing, and termination of pregnancies in women who are HIV positive.

HIV has exposed, also, the low priority given to research about women's health needs. Although, in many parts of the world, equal numbers of women and men are infected by HIV, research on how HIV affects women has been only a very recent concern. Even now, very few resources are being directed towards understanding the ways the disease affects women. Earlier research was directed towards the effects on *children* born to HIV-infected mothers. And nearly a decade into the HIV 'epidemic', a first international conference about women was called 'The Effects of AIDS on the Mother and the Child'.

Currently women appear to be diagnosed late or misdiagnosed or even not diagnosed at all. Part of the reason for this is historic: the research on the progression of the virus has been based on information collected from active service users – who were mainly North American and European white gay men. Therefore, the illnesses and symptoms that presently define 'HIV symptomatic' and 'AIDS' categories are drawn from the illnesses in men.

The implications of this are great: (1) it leads to the exclusion of women from important treatment and services that could enable them to have healthier and longer lives; (2) it also means that women remain invisible or visible in such small numbers that they remain 'statistically insignificant' and therefore discounted; and (3) the true picture of HIV within the population is distorted, affecting how prevention information is being offered, where HIV research is directed, and what will be the health and service needs (for governmental planning and budgeting).

There are much greater numbers of women affected by HIV in the United States than in Britain, and some USA research on patterns of HIV infection in women is beginning to be reported. The results are very alarming: 48 per cent of women die of HIV infection before they can officially be given an AIDS diagnosis (Chu, 1990); women appear to live a much shorter time after diagnosis than men; black women and poor women are disproportionally affected (these last two issues must be seen, of course, within the bigger picture of women's socio-economic situations within society, as stated before); there appear to be patterns of illnesses and conditions (due to HIV's damaging the body's immune system) that are specific to women's reproductive systems, and others appear more often in women than in men but these illnesses and conditions are not part of the current AIDS and HIV definitions.

These research findings raise important questions that need to be addressed:

(1) At present the epidemiology of HIV, the movement of HIV through the human population throughout the world, is interpreted through the *number of people with an AIDS diagnosis*. And, on this information, governments and departments of health base their planning and budgeting for services and support.

'AIDS' is a complicated medical definition, determined initially and still strongly controlled by the United States Centers for Disease Control, along with the World Health Organization. 'AIDS' is a carefully defined collection of life-threatening illnesses and conditions in connexion with HIV. Yet women are dying before they have the 'correct' illnesses. Can the AIDS definition be complete? Are women presenting with different life-threatening diseases than men? What are the reasons why women are dying sooner than men?

(2) HIV symptoms and conditions are also carefully defined. Yet this definition includes no conditions that are specific to women. And

medical practitioners are not noticing indicators of HIV infection in women. Can the HIV classification be complete? What should the medical profession be looking for, to insure earlier recognition of HIV infection in women?

The initial information, alarming as it is, needs to be understood in a British context as well as in every other country. Therefore, the following questions need urgently to be addressed in Britain, through Department of Health statistics collection and through research:

(1) Do women die more rapidly after receiving an AIDS diagnosis than men? If so, why?

(2) What are the causes of death in women who are infected by HIV? Do these fit into the current definition of AIDS? Does this definition need to be altered?

(3) Some patterns are already emerging about women-specific HIV health problems, e.g., vaginal candidiasis (thrush) and preindicators to cervical cancer. What is the picture, the 'natural history', of HIV in women? How does HIV affect women differently from men? What are women-specific HIV-related illnesses and conditions? Are there conditions that are more prevalent in women than in men?

(4) What are the transmission risks around woman-to-woman transmission? Are statistics being collected to measure this?

(5) How do women have access to drug trials? What gender comparisons are made, on these drug trials? Are drugs safe for women, if tested only on men?

To answer all these questions, further investigation and research is urgently needed. And support from women and women's organizations is much needed, to press for the resources to make this happen. As an example, in Britain there is presently a research proposal to the Medical Research Council (MRC) for a long-term study of the natural history of HIV in women. One of the issues (problems) appears to be financing. Will the MRC give the necessary funding to this long-term women-specific HIV research (the *only* one in Britain)? Will the 'social-cultural' aspect of the research be included?

A group of women from the Women's HIV/AIDS Network in England and Wales has formed to begin to address these questions. Any questions, contributions or support would be welcome, and can be sent via: Emily Scharf, 40 Milton Park, London N6 5QA.

Notes

Emily Scharf is involved in the HIV field in the voluntary and statutory sector, and is presently working freelance in HIV training and development.

Sue Toole is a social work manager in a specialist HIV and AIDS team in an inner London borough.

Reference

CHU, S. et al. (1990) 'Impact of the Human Immunodeficiency Virus on Mortality in Women of Reproductive Age, United States' *Journal of the American Medical Association* 11 July, Vol. 254, No. 4, pp. 225–9.

LESBIANS EVOLVING HEALTH CARE:
Cancer and AIDS

Jackie Winnow

One of our local newspapers recently ran an article addressing the plight of the 100 women with AIDS in the San Francisco Bay Area (Ginsburg, 1989). According to the article, the local community had responded by starting many different sorts of services for these women: housing, child care, a day-care centre, haircuts, a food bank, massage, counselling, meals and other support services.

At the same time (1988), there were approximately 40,000 women living in the Bay Area with cancer. At least 4,000 of them were lesbians. In that same year, 8,000 women were newly diagnosed with cancer, and 4,000 women in the San Francisco Bay Area died from cancer (Austin, 1985).

The 40,000 women with cancer don't have the services available to the 100 women with AIDS. Certainly the women with AIDS should have their services, but the very existence of those services brings into sharp focus another problem.

I am both a cancer activist and an AIDS activist. As a lesbian feminist, I have been involved with the AIDS crisis since the early 1980s. In 1985 I was diagnosed with breast cancer, founded the Women's Cancer Resource Center in Berkeley, California in 1986, and was diagnosed with metastatic breast cancer in my lungs and bones in 1988. I have lost friends, acquaintances and colleagues to cancer and to AIDS. Both of these diseases are life-threatening, and yet I have seen my community rally around one and overlook the other.

As a feminist, I know the importance of putting discussion in a historical perspective. Without that perspective, we cannot remember our intent or hold on to our vision. Without it, we cannot remember where we've been or where we're going. Without it, we lose our own political perspective and become pawns on other people's agendas.

Throughout history, the issue of women's health has been closely related to the standing of women as healers, or caregivers, as we are now called. It is interesting to note that the term 'caregivers' seems to have replaced 'healers', a substitution which echoes the current status of women and reflects how we think of ourselves today.

Lesbians have been in the vanguard of the current women's and lesbian/gay liberation movements and have held uncomfortable places in both. In the Women's Liberation movement, lesbians have been suspect for being lesbian, and in the gay/lesbian movement, suspect for being women. Our needs, if noticed at all, are placed on the back burners of the agenda-makers. We were always the other in the lesbian/gay and women's movements, although we were often the exciting and driving energy in both.

I began to work on the AIDS crisis in 1982 when AIDS hysteria endangered our civil rights, increased anti-lesbian/gay violence, divided our community over the bathhouse and sexuality issues, and increased discrimination, particularly in the area of employment. AIDS hysteria and misinformation caused great numbers of men – in a community of people already considered to be pariahs – to question their gayness, their sexuality and their self-esteem. While little was firmly known about the cause or transmission of AIDS, it was clear that large numbers of gay men were getting it, and that our survival as a people depended on our response. And we, the lesbian/gay community, reacted admirably – with vigour, courage and caring.

As a community, we had never before received much funding for any of our organizations or services. Much of our early organizing was grass-roots, and we had little concrete experience for what was to come, though our past work laid a solid foundation upon which to respond to this crisis. From next to nothing, we created services that educated the lesbian/gay and general communities, housed people with AIDS/ARC, served them meals, provided emotional and practical support and provided funds. We created model programmes for hospital care, hospice care, and social services. We demanded government responsiveness, fought for good legislation, and continue to fight tirelessly against bad legislation and bigotry. We created information services on various treatments and ways to access them. We honoured the dead through the creation of an evolving monument, the AIDS quilt.

And this terrible disease opened our hearts to love and an incredible, enduring sadness while we continued to go on. All this from a community of people who had come to exist as a community a mere fifteen to twenty years ago.

With the advent of AIDS funding, the lesbian/gay community suddenly found itself running multimillion-dollar organizations, and an AIDS establishment was built. The AIDS/ARC crisis and its ensuing organizations became the lesbian/gay movement, and nearly all other issues took second stage. Indeed, the leaders of the AIDS establishment became the leaders of the lesbian/gay movement, some of whom were not even lesbians or gay men, but experts in AIDS. Not surprisingly,

AIDS took priority over all our other needs as lesbians and gay men. Since the crisis was building rapidly and the need to respond was immediate, there was little analysis of the implications of our choices and actions. Where the money came from or the caveats for its use were issues rarely addressed, and connexions to deficiencies in the health- and social-service systems affecting the larger community were generally ignored.

Response to the AIDS crisis has had an enormous impact on lesbians. Many of us involved in the women's movement turned our attentions to the lesbian/gay movement. There were many reasons for this shift. AIDS is a clear, delineated crisis, and there is an urgent need to help people in our community. Women, even lesbians, were raised to be caregivers in general and caregivers to men in particular. And even though lesbians have made a conscious choice to disown that heritage, we have none the less incorporated many of its basic tenets.

While there have always been unaddressed and painful divisions between lesbians and gay men, coming to the service of men around the issue of AIDS served finally to validate our existence. We could work with relative safety because, by and large, we don't get AIDS, our lovers won't get AIDS, nor will our lesbian neighbours. We can even, sometimes, work in a queer environment. The work structures are set out for us; the funding is available. And AIDS is something the whole society is addressing; we can actually fit in, be considered heroic, important, decent, and be recognized for it. We get to work where our hearts lie.

This is not to say that working in AIDS is easy, or that we don't care about the people we know with AIDS. It is to say that we are making excruciating choices without even being aware of them.

While the women's movement still pulses with creativity and excitement, many of the institutions, services and political agendas have disappeared. No one takes care of women or lesbians except women or lesbians, and we have a hard time taking care of ourselves, of finding ourselves worthy and important enough for attention. We are told that the process of change is a slow and plodding one. But we know that only when concerns are taken seriously does action follow.

As a woman with cancer, I have had to come face to face with how serious the situation is for women with cancer in our community; I have had to learn about what we need and what we don't have – the hard way. When I was waiting for my first biopsy result in May of 1985, I remember sitting in a Lesbian/Gay Advisory Committee meeting of the San Francisco Human Rights Commission. Our meeting focused on AIDS, and I remember thinking – screaming internally, really – what about me?

I had a lumpectomy followed by radiation. I survived, and was expected to go back to my life and my work, to work on AIDS. If you have AIDS, you can go to the AIDS Foundation for food and social services advocacy; you can receive emergency funding through the AIDS Emergency Fund; you can get excellent meals through Project Open

Hand. Your animals are taken care of should you land in the hospital or become too sick to care for them yourself. There are clinics, alternative centres, and organizations fighting for drugs and research and mental-health needs of people with AIDS.

But if you have cancer, you wait endlessly for a support group. And if you are a lesbian, a woman of colour, working class, and/or believe in alternative approaches to treating cancer, you don't fit into the few groups that are available. No organization shepherds you through the social-service maze. No group brings you luscious meals or sends support people to clean your house or hold your hand.

Ignoring the needs of people with cancer is more typical of our culture. We live in a society which by and large does not take care of its sick. When people in our community suffer pain and deprivation, hardly anyone seems to give a damn. In the case of AIDS, however, we have – as a community – built a model of social response to a crisis, but a model which has not been replicated outside of AIDS.

Cancer, like AIDS, is about living. It's about living with a life-threatening disease, in whatever state, in whatever condition. As an activist, I have learned that action and change take place through collective support. My own cancer experience has strengthened my belief that all disease and illness are not only physiological, but also political.

I took some of what I learned in AIDS work and much of what I learned from feminist organizing and Women's Liberation, and together with other women created the Women's Cancer Resource Center. We desperately needed a resource, support and advocacy centre where women with cancer could be empowered to make their own choices and be supported by other women – a centre controlled by women with cancer. I knew this vision was possible because the models had already been built for AIDS, as well as in the women's community.

The Women's Cancer Resource Center (WCRC) has been slow to grow, partly because some of us who have, or have had, cancer need to spend most of our energies taking care of our health. Many women are no longer involved in organizing work, but instead have turned their energies into working solely on themselves. Most of the remaining activists' energy is going into the fight against AIDS. Further, the WCRC is not in the closet about having lesbians on the advisory committee, nor – though we are an agency which serves all women with cancer – are we quiet about offering services to lesbians. Consequently, the homophobia of our society prevents us from receiving much in the way of funding, and those funding agencies which are not deterred by homophobia consider that they have sufficiently funded efforts on behalf of lesbian/gay people when they give money to AIDS projects.

Even with all these obstacles, WCRC has blossomed and flourished. The advisory committee worked on funding and programming; we began a drop-in support group; we presented forums and educationals; we started information sources on referrals and counselling; we produced successful fundraisers; we found and organized an office from which we can work and into which we can welcome all women with cancer who need help and support.

Then I found another lump in my breast. There were further tests, revealing that the cancer had spread to my lungs and bones. I could not believe that I was so ill. I had been exercising, feeling great, working long hours just as I had before the initial diagnosis. Despite my shock, however, I was not really surprised. Somehow I knew; I understood the precariousness of good health. Cancer had never been that far from my mind. And now, here it was again. For a time I fell apart, knowing the implications of this spread, knowing women who had metastatic breast cancer, knowing women who had died.

Finally I made my decisions. I used what I had learned over the past three years as a cancer activist and also what I had learned as an AIDS activist and feminist. I agonized over every choice as I went through my treatments and did my research. But I lived with a great deal of support from my lover, Teya, and from friends and acquaintances. These people I love. I cannot always express the extent of that love, but it is very present, and it gives me extreme pleasure as well as extreme pain.

One evening at my house, for instance, my acupuncturist was giving me treatment, a friend had gone food shopping and was putting the food away, a third friend was washing vegetables for juicing, and still another had just brought me a macrobiotic meal. The feelings of love I had for these people were indescribable, but at the same time I wished my friends weren't there. I wished they could be doing something else, that they were not there because I needed them so much. With the first diagnosis, my life's axis permanently tilted; with this diagnosis, I live constantly on the edge.

But we who must battle cancer need more than our friends. We need knowledge and resources. Just as we were women and experts in our fields in the Middle Ages, so we need to lay claim to our heritage now. We have many people in nascent stages of expertise, but not enough experts. When we started the women's health movement, we began by taking control of our reproductive and gynaecological health care. Now we need specialists in cancer, lupus, arthritis, environmental illness. We need practitioners in allopathic medicine, Chinese medicine, homeopathy, chiropractic. Lesbians can't afford to go to a 'regular' doctor hoping for someone who is not homophobic. An oncology nurse at a recent forum on women and cancer reminded us that just because doctors have become aware of gay men due to AIDS, we can't assume they are less homophobic when they deal with lesbians. We need practitioners who are experts in their fields and clinics which are supportive of us as lesbians.

When lesbians get sick, we also get poor. Women are on a low rung of the financial ladder, and when we become ill, the bottom falls out much quicker because we are closer to it. We lose our health insurance and can't get more. If we are lucky enough to have a job, we have to stay in it. Many women I know work in situations where working feels almost physically unbearable because they can't afford to do anything else.

Some of us who are unemployed would love to work, but no one will hire us. Some of us who are sick receive SSI payments but are hardly making it since, cruelly, the amount is so low.

One of the reasons that AIDS has become 'different' from other diseases is because of the community organizing around it. Although diseases such as cancer have not yet had that kind of organized community support, we need to examine the information we are given about cancer with an eye towards its politics. There are politics in everything.

Cancer has had the American Cancer Society controlling information about the disease and controlling all the resources in the fight against it. The people on the board of the American Cancer Society, as well as other cancer institutions, are people with a lot of power in this society – power to maintain the status quo, thereby keeping themselves in power. Often they are representatives of chemical and pharmaceutical companies and the very scientists who stand to gain wealth and power from cancer research, and that research is geared to big bucks, not to actual prevention.

Real prevention would mean changing fundamental social structures. It would mean going after the tobacco industry, stopping the pollution of our environment, providing quality food. But when the medical profession talks about prevention, they mean at best small, individual acts – like stopping smoking and reducing dietary fat intake. When they talk about prevention, they talk about early detection methods like mammograms or breast self-examination. But once a tumor is found in your breast, you already have cancer, raising the question about whether early detection actually lengthens survival rates or simply lengthens the time you know you have cancer.

When a study came out a few years ago asserting that breast self-examination was meaningless, (*San Francisco Chronicle*, 1987) I was furious. Most women I know with breast cancer had found their cancer through breast exams. When doctors talk about early detection and admonish patients for not coming in sooner, they imply that an earlier appointment might have meant a cure would have been possible. Yet many women walk around with lumps in their breasts for a long time and go from doctor to doctor being repeatedly told that it's nothing, that it's 'just fibrocystic breasts', that they will 'watch it'. I have known women who died fairly quickly after a diagnosis of breast cancer because their concerns about lumps in their breasts were ignored by doctors, and they were able to get attention only when their cancer had become quite advanced.

Groups facing health crises are often pitted against each other, and it is important for us to understand the reasons for those divisions. Many people with cancer are upset about the attention paid to AIDS. This inequality is not the fault of the people with AIDS, but rather of the systems that create the divisions. People start fighting over the same piece of the pie. It is not an accident.

Recently there was a report in the press about the AIDS crisis decimating funding for the National Cancer Institute, as the money was being taken from cancer research and going to AIDS. It wasn't taken from the military budget or the space budget. So the researchers in various diseases compete with each other, and consequently people who have the diseases do the same thing. Government and corporate researchers not only have not found a cure for cancer, but they continue to allow its spread while remaining apparently unwilling to offer adequate services to people who have cancer.

We need money for both cancer and AIDS. And we need a National Cancer Institute that does relevant research, not research into a quick cure that costs a fortune. Instead we need real prevention, real cure. We all know that pollution causes cancer, but the NCI and the American Cancer Society do nothing about the root causes of the disease. Just as we question what is said about AIDS, we need to question what is said about cancer, or any other disease.

Earlier in the women's movement, we took what had victimized us – rape, battery, incest – and worked toward changing society while making ourselves stronger. Now we tend to work only on ourselves individually; we do not make connexions to the world, nor do we see that the world should change. Much of our energy is now put into therapy work, but without changing the environment which fosters victimization, that exploitation is allowed to continue. In that vein, a new disease model has emerged which holds that the individual is responsible for her illness.

We are a culture obsessed with looks and with health. The sort of thinking exemplified by the fitness craze rests on a faulty premise – the postulate that one's health is totally within the control of the individual. This premise presupposes that we create our own reality and that we have ultimate freedom of choice and total control over our own destinies.

When I first got out of the hospital, I opened a gay newspaper to find a positive review of a book called *The Silent Wound* (Boyd, 1984). The book was about how women get breast cancer because of repressed sexuality and conflicting new roles. Just like intellectuals get brain cancer? But beyond the nonsense put forth in the book, what really angered me was that a progressive newspaper in our community was lauding such nonsense as being enlightened, when all it did was feed into the notion of women's passivity and the individualization and psychological basis of disease.

I cannot count the number of people who have told me that I must not have had a positive attitude, for if I had I would not have gotten cancer. This pronouncement is cruel. I have also been told never to get angry because anger, too, is bad. I have been told that I worked too hard, thereby taking too much stress upon myself. Such thinking reflects a society which does not want us to be angry, which does not want us to be activists. We need to resist this sort of tranquillizer; instead, we need to ask why our culture wants to lull us into submission.

Not only do we fall prey to the emotional-causation nonsense, we are told that faulty spirituality causes cancer. The Puritans used to think that money was a sign of God's grace, and now we have come to think that health is such a sign. We have courses in miracles and karma, showing us, if we are ill, that something we have done in the past is causing our troubles now; we are working out our karma . . . what goes around comes around. Is that why women are raped and black people lynched? Karma? Such beliefs take the onus off the perpetrator, allow us to accept the unacceptable, forgive the unforgivable.

We have also romanticized death. Death is not lovely, not easy, most often not wanted. Romanticizing death makes it acceptable and welcome. We are excused from the struggle against wrongful death from a rotting planet and a society which has its priorities turned around.

We live in a world with acid rain, with a hole in the ozone layer, where food is mass produced and picked early with no nutrients, where pesticides are sprayed on the workers and the food we eat, where the animals we eat are raised in a tortured environment and fed hormones and antibiotics. We live in a world that has chemical dumps under housing tracts, schools, and playgrounds. We live in a society that has nuclear reactors and nuclear dumps and nuclear waste and nuclear bombs that go off over us and underground, where winds spread the invisible molecules and atoms everywhere. We call it pollution. It is invisible violence.

Society must change and redirect itself to be life-affirming, where welfare and health care are respected, where profits don't count more than people, where we are free of chemical and radiation hazards, where good food is available, where each person is recognized as significant and worthy of life.

As women, we need to see ourselves again as healers. We need to see the interconnexions of all these issues, to take the skills we have learned as feminists and apply them to our work in AIDS and our work with women. And then take the skills we have gotten from working in AIDS and apply them to women's health care. Let's bring it back home.

I have wondered whether the urgency I feel comes from the fact that I have cancer. But I think that my cancer has only served to bring my sense of urgency closer to me. I firmly believe that we are on the brink of disaster, and that we must be very forceful if we are to stop the destruction before there is no 'us'. We have to stop being nice girls and start fighting as though our lives depended on it. Because they do.

Notes

Jackie Winnow was born in New York and lived in Oakland, California. She was the founder of the Women's Cancer Resource Center in Berkeley and was the coordinator of the Lesbian/Gay and AIDS Unit of the San Francisco Human Rights Commission. Jackie died in November 1991. Her work continues at the Women's Cancer Resource Center.

This article is adapted from a speech given as the keynote address to the Lesbian Caregivers and the AIDS Epidemic Conference, January 1989. It is published in the collection *1 in 3. Women with Cancer confront an Epidemic* edited by Judy Brady and published by Cleis Press: San Francisco. ISBN 0 939416 49 2. Published by kind permission of Cleis Press.

References

AUSTIN Donald F. (1985) *Cancer in California: Cancer Incidence Rates for the San Francisco-Oakland Metropolitan Statistical Area 1980–1984, Technical Report No. 1*, Cancer Prevention Section and California Tumor Registry, California Department of Health Services, p. 6. Figures are adapted for 1988.

BOYD, Peggy (1984) *The Silent Wound* Reading, Massachusetts: Addison-Wesley.

GINSBURG, Marsha (1989) 'More Women Battle AIDS' *San Francisco Chronicle* 1 January, pp. A1, A20.

SAN FRANCISCO CHRONICLE (1987) 'Study Questions Self-Exams for Breast Cancer' 24 April, p. 1.

AIDS REVIEW: Inventing AIDS

Lynne Segal

Inventing AIDS by Cindy Patton, London: Routledge, 1991, £9.99 Pbk, ISBN 0 415 90257 6.

Ignorance, fear, brutality and neglect are not the main themes of this new book on AIDS, but something a little more insidious: the liberal and above all scientific discourses of AIDS. It is here, as well as in the many more obvious abuses, that power, discrimination, homophobia, racism and prejudice reside. It is good to see a new book from Cindy Patton, one of the leading and most tireless activists, thinkers and writers about AIDS in the US. Her earlier book, *Sex and Germs* (South End Press), back in 1985, was one of the first and clearest attempts to sort out the biological, psychological, social and political issues surrounding the HIV virus, and the orchestrated epidemic of fear and hatred with which so many responded to it, as well as one of the first to broadcast gay and lesbian resistance and practices of safe sex in the USA. In her most recent book, Patton moves on to consider the apparently more progressive responses of 'the AIDS service industry' in the US, suggesting that the strictly 'scientific' approach it adopts has led to serious weaknesses in its educational strategies, as well as further discrimination against gays, women and black people.

From the mid-1980s in the USA, Patton argues, the newly emerging government-funded and professionalized AIDS services began to dominate and erase from public knowledge the former history of AIDS activism, initiated largely by gay communities, and to a lesser extent IV drug-taking communities, between 1981 and 1985. This new AIDS industry emerging in the US, with its own goals and perspectives based on ideas of 'victims', 'volunteers' and 'experts', contrasted sharply with the earlier politicized and self-empowering AIDS activism. In the new AIDS industry, care for people with AIDS replicated the existing irrational delivery of health care in the USA, relying on volunteers and charity work, and deepening class and race discriminations – now greatly exacerbated by Reaganite cuts in social services. For example, rewriting AIDS activism as altruism, meant both diffusing the political significance of community organizing, by promoting the 'good works' of gay male volunteers and the white middle-class women who tended to work with them, and blaming black and drug-using 'communities' for failing to provide for their own care.

Patton also criticizes what she sees as the weaknesses of the new professional AIDS-education policies. Between 1985 and 1989, for example, government-funded AIDS education was directed not at those, like drug users, most immediately vulnerable to HIV infection, but at those, like students, most likely to accept the middle-class view of AIDS as a tragic disease which medicine would one day cure. More significantly, rather than emphasizing the importance of safer-sex practices, illustrating their possible diversity and pleasures, and rather than promoting safe drug-taking routines, professional programmes in the US have concentrated instead on encouraging the idea of 'voluntary' HIV antibody testing as its primary educational strategy for dealing with AIDS. This is even though, Patton adds, widespread testing programmes have been internationally widely rejected as expensive, ineffective and misleading as an educational strategy.

One central theme of Patton's analysis is thus that professionalized education programmes have ignored the success of earlier AIDS activists which suggest the long-term value of participatory projects, with local groups generating their own strategies and thus changing behaviour as a form of resistance and community building. Instead, emphasis is placed on more neutral strategies like widespread testing programmes and the idea that information, *by itself*, will generate behaviour change. Yet there is now 'general scientific consensus' that there is no predictable relationship even between knowledge of HIV antibody status and behaviour change. Moreover, when 'safe sex' is promoted by the new professional groups, it loses the inventiveness and creativity which gay men had invested in it as a positive sexual choice, clearly indicating those practices which are risky and those many other sexual practices which are safe. Safer sex becomes instead merely reference to condom use and reduction in number of partners. Especially with its targeting of heterosexual groups in 1986/7, the professional literature on 'safe sex', rather than challenging vaginal intercourse as 'the sex act', reduced all sex to penile performance – with or without condoms. Meanwhile the passing of discriminatory laws like the Helms Amendment has meant a prohibition on government funding for *any* sex-positive education, and increased levels of homophobia in the US.

The scientific biases of the AIDS industry have thus involved the remedicalization of sexuality in professional AIDS discourses which, in the process, still rely upon all the old conventional gendered and racist paradigms and metaphors of sex. Studying the literature on AIDS in

Africa, for instance, Patton exposes both its dependence on centuries of stereotyped racist perception, constructing 'African AIDS' as something altogether different, more virulent and terrifying than AIDS in the West, and enabling callous and unethical use of African subjects for empirical testing procedures. Yet Patton is not without some optimism, despite what she sees as the lethal failures of Western science when educating people about AIDS to provide useful practical advice about either sex or drugs:

> There are, despite all this, some very exciting projects underway in communities disenfranchised by the white middle-class AIDS industry – in communities of color, among IV drug users, among sex workers, in communities in post-colonial and post-revolutionary nations. These projects rely on community involvement, are open-ended, and view the *process* of AIDS education as important in determining how AIDS will be perceived and how well behavior changes will succeed. But these projects are under funded and in danger of the absorption which homogenised the earlier projects by and for the gay male community.

One disappointment of her book for feminists is that Patton frequently mentions, but rarely focuses sufficiently directly upon, the specific gender issues around HIV/AIDS discourse and safer-sex practices. For example, she says clearly enough that safer-sex practices in gay male cultures can work because they assume a rough equality between sexual partners – both could be equally responsible for ensuring safer sex occurred, an assumption which clearly cannot be made for heterosexual couplings. But Patton does not explore more fully how women can work to overcome this in their own educational programmes or individual and collective practices. A theme for her next book, perhaps? Meanwhile, there is plenty to chew over in this one.

AIDS REVIEW: Women and Health in Africa

Alice Henry

Women and Health in Africa, edited by Meredith Turshen, Africa World Press, Inc., PO Box 1892, Trenton NJ 08607, 1991. US$14.95 ISBN 0 865431817

Meredith Turshen has collected articles reflecting the complex health problems of African women within the broad context of war and revolution, economic and work issues, and population growth as well as looking at 'just' health, and health programmes. Many of the articles are based on field research done by African people (some men) now writing or studying abroad. Here is a report on just one, but an exemplary one.

'Gender, Power and Risk of AIDS in Zaire' is a report on a CONNAISSIDA action research by Brooke Grundfest Schoepf, Walu Engundu, Rukarangira Wa Nkera and Claude Schoepf. CONNAIS-SIDA was set up to understand how AIDS affects the people of Kinshasa and Lumumbashi, Zaire's two largest cities with a combined population of more than four and one-half million, and the causes, including cultural ones, which affect the spread of infection.

In Zaire, and the rest of Africa, AIDS is primarily transmitted by heterosexual sex. Contamination of the blood supply is another import-ant factor, especially affecting women because blood transfusion after illegal abortion is all too common. In 1986, infection levels were reported to be between 6 and 9 per cent among sexually active urban adults, but in some East African cities up to 30 per cent test positive for HIV. In this situation, prevention involves convincing everyone that 'normal', 'natu-ral', everyday patterns of sexual behaviour must change. Unfortu-nately, there is nowhere in the world where knowing the facts is enough to change sexual behaviour. By mid-1987 almost all of six hundred adults and teenagers interviewed understood AIDS to be a fatal disease, transmitted by sexual relations and exchange of blood. But one fact that could help change behaviour was missing; most did not know what a condom was.

The authors point out that disease epidemics often erupt in times of war, and economic crisis certainly makes public health measures against spread of disease difficult. Zaire has been hit by bad international trade conditions and a heavy burden of debt. Since publication of the article, rebellion against Mobutu's rule has hit the headlines, leading even the US to question his dictatorial methods.

The authors go on to say that women have a particularly hard time economically, although men too find few paid jobs in the recorded economy. Most women were and are confined to raising crops and children; when they move to cities they support themselves through petty trade and services – food preparation, sewing, smuggling, making beer and alcohol, and sexual services.

Some of the complexity of sexual exchanges are captured by the authors:

> Several forms of stable multiple partnerships are linked to informal sector activities and may contribute to the spread of AIDS. For example, male long distance traders are likely to have several wives or women with whom they live in relatively stable unions in towns along their routes. Wives and children provide the trader with an identity as a responsible adult with a reason for being in the town. Wives make trading contacts and obtain permits using their local kinship and patron-client networks. They also may trade on their own account with goods or capital supplied by the visiting husband. Some wives are monogamous; others have two or more husbands.
>
> Women traders are perceived by many men as universally promiscuous. Since they are able to command their own resources, their sexuality is beyond male control. Women who are not deterred by moral scruples can use sexual strategies to economic advantage. Some develop regular sexual relationships with officials to facilitate obtaining permits and fee waivers.

In fact, it's risky to engage in any irregular trade unless you have political protection.

It's no surprise to find that sex and living arrangements are thoroughly entangled with economic exchanges and mutual support. It would be ridiculous to try to stop sexual trading in Zaire or anywhere else, so instead, CONNAISSIDA looked at how to overcome the constraints that make condom use difficult.

Their first workshops, addressed to women living in a low-income community, used role play, group discussion and other active learning methods to show women they could reduce the risk of getting AIDS. In October 1987, a network of fifteen sex workers asked CONNAISSIDA for information on how to prevent AIDS. The women had known for some time that their activities put them at risk, but they had no other way to support themselves so felt they couldn't do anything about it. But recently their neighbours had begun to make hostile comments about them being 'disease distributors' – a result of the national mass-media campaign.

The examples of how the sessions were run might help other AIDS educators. They included other community-health issues related to AIDS to defuse the stigma attached to sexual transmission, talking about ways to prevent malaria so fewer anaemic children would need blood transfusions. They explained how needles should be sterilized, or thrown away if they're the disposable type. Although drug injection isn't a common way of transmitting AIDs in Zaire, hospital transfusions are, and this demonstration gave the women a way to check on hygiene standards at their local dispensary.

They held a whole session on condoms, trying to make women comfortable with a largely uncongenial, unnatural and foreign technology. They put condoms on cola bottles, broke a few, and talked about how to get them on the men. They then took some home so they could bring back reports on success and failure.

The local Protestant Mothers Club learned about the workshops for sex workers and asked CONNAISSIDA to hold some workshops for them. This also involved 'condom seduction', expertly performed by a grandmother who used to be a professional sex worker, playing the reluctant husband, and a young sex worker, a member of the congregation, who played the cajoling wife. This wasn't a set-up by the project workers; in fact, it brought home to them the fluidity between 'prostitutes', 'mothers' and 'church members'.

Follow-ups three months after the sessions found that all but one of the sex workers were using condoms. (The non-user said she had genital sores that made condoms an impossible pain, so the project workers drove her to the hospital for treatment as the local dispensary had no testing facilities.) It seemed that knowing about condoms raised women's prestige; clients liked them knowing about prevention. But six months later, condom use went down from 'almost always' to 'sometimes'. Student clients told them their condoms were outdated; they wanted the more attractive product distributed by the Social Marketing Project. Even worse, *Paris Match* had run an article by US sex researcher Jonathan Kolodney, who said that condoms are not completely protective. The students thought this meant that condoms were useless, and told the sex workers, 'No need to use those things!' The sex workers didn't want to lose the relatively high-status student customers and hadn't heard any new messages about AIDS. They didn't have radios or TVs, so couldn't hear the message of the Public Health Department's AIDS coordinator who went on TV to promote condoms – and the students were inclined to believe the authority of *Paris Match*.

Women's power relative to men was also an issue for the churchwomen. The husbands of twenty of the sixty participants refused point blank to use condoms or discuss the risk of AIDS. Some husbands with multiple partners were angry and threatening. One husband refused to give his partner the monthly housekeeping allowance and told her to go hustle for it. Another twenty at least had a discussion with their partner, but were persuaded their risks were minimal. In this group, both partners said they had not had any other partner for the past few years. The last twenty said their husbands agreed, at least in principle, to use condoms. The researchers weren't sure about actual practice, and intended to find some way of getting anonymous self-reports.

There were several other reactions that would also slow the spread of AIDS. The churchwomen asked for workshops for husbands and young adults in their households, showing that young people can be reached through their family, even if older family members aren't happy directly talking about sex issues with the younger set.

Both sex workers and women in the church group asked for help in getting treatment for symptoms of sexually transmitted disease. Genital ulcers help the spread of AIDS; there were no treatment facilities close by. There seemed to be little chance of opening a clinic; the project provided transportation to the nearest centre.

The groups agreed that what women most needed were ways to make money so they didn't have to depend on men and have to provide sexual services to multiple men in order to survive. The women had tried many ways to enlarge their family resources, but with little luck. They had not yet come up with a realistic plan of cooperative action.

The massive resistance to practical responses is illustrated by the following example. The church mothers club organized a banquet for participants and health trainers; the minister spoke, informing them that AIDS is divine retribution for sins; the righteous need not fear infection. The Protestant bishop had also recently mouthed similar platitudes.

CONNAISSIDA concludes that women cannot effect change all by themselves; surely just distributing condoms to sex workers (a government suggestion) will have little impact in a situation where 10 to 30 per cent of sexually active men and women test positive for HIV. They suggest that men, especially high-status men, have to change their ways.

> Culturally appropriate empowering education is one necessary but not
> sufficient part of AIDS prevention, or of any health and development
> strategy. The limited long-term success of CONNAISSIDA's experiment
> with sex workers and churchwomen is a reminder that communication
> systems are social systems and exhibit the same hierarchically structured
> patterns as the wider society.

Exactly. AIDS control means increasing the economic and social status of women, and not even a brilliant action-research programme like CONNAISSIDA can do that. Nevertheless, Brooke Schoepf and her co-authors give a good model of how to report the specifics of AIDS intervention, and several of their actions can give ideas to AIDS activists in any country.

NOW IS THE TIME FOR FEMINIST CRITICISM: A Review of *Asinamali!*

Carol Steinberg

Introduction

South African drama of the 1980s is characterized by its powerful and creative attack on apartheid. In a time in which the voices of many black South Africans were silenced through the banning of their political organizations, drama became a crucial means of public political expression.

The political role of anti-apartheid drama cannot be underestimated. During the difficult years of its performance it was perhaps inappropriate to criticize it. In the face of the harsh conditions of theatre production, the ever-vigilant censors, and the detention and assassination of theatre workers, the imperative of progressive drama critics was to encourage anti-apartheid drama almost unequivocally.

One of the most renowned genres, or subgenres, of anti-apartheid drama is the minimalist protest/resistance theatre that reached a peak during the early to mid-1980s. This subgenre may be defined by its workshop method of production; its all black male cast; its minimalist sets and costume; its high-energy performance using song, dance and mime; its use of the images of the South Africa of the eighties: the freedom song, the slogans, the toyi-toyi, the necklace, the Albert Street queue, etc. These plays took as their themes the hardships that black South Africans suffer under apartheid and their resistance to it. Plays like *Woza Albert, Asinamali!, Bopha* and worker plays like *The Long March* form part of this subgenre.[1]

In the early 1990s apartheid is by no means dead and repression continues, but the post 2 February 1990 era undoubtedly extends the space in which cultural activists can think and work. Albie Sachs's recent controversial intervention articulates and argues for this space.[2]

It is time to interrogate a canon which many of us hold very dear: anti-apartheid theatre. It has always been incumbent on feminist cultural critics to interrogate their own canon. A revisionary criticism of the gender ideology of the Anglo-American canon forms a significant component of the feminist critical tradition. While South African drama critics move away from 'solidarity criticism', it is time for feminist drama critics in particular to refuse the notion of a genderless class and race subjectivity.

The position I argue in this instance is a 'weak' one in terms of feminist cultural criticism. Via an analysis of Mbongeni Ngema's[3] *Asinamali!* (1986), I will attempt to demonstrate that the gender ideology of the play detracts from its imperative to mobilize against racism. I will not argue that the play should address women's issues and struggles directly, but simply that its gender ideology undermines its motive force – the struggle against apartheid, and that to this extent, the play fails in its own terms.

While I recognize that sexual oppression has a material existence that cannot be reduced to an ancillary of other forms of oppression, I am not prepared to assert that *all* plays should directly address women's issues. Sexual oppression must be fought concurrently with other struggles, but this does not translate into the contention that all plays, books and films must address sexual oppression.

In the dramatic world of *Asinamali!* a bold line is drawn between 'us' and 'them': those audience members who share the life experiences and world view of the five central characters and those who don't. This dynamic 'sustain(s) different and conflicting [actor-audience] relationships within a single audience simultaneously' (Banning, 1989: 193). It is on this actor-audience relationship that my paper will focus. Like the other plays in its genre, one of *Asinamali!*'s primary imperatives is the mobilization of the 'us' members of the audience against racial, and to a lesser extent, class oppression. If, as I will argue, the play delimits the 'us' audience members to an exclusive group of black men, then black women are alienated and excluded. By relegating black women to the 'them' category of whites and informers, the play reduces the target of its mobilizatory force, thereby undermining its antiracist imperative.[4]

Background to *Asinamali!*

A new phase of resistance to apartheid began in 1984 with an explosion of mass anger erupting in the townships of the Vaal Triangle. Residents marched in opposition to rent increases. There were physical attacks on the community councillors responsible, and some were killed. The uprisings soon spread around the country. The state responded with increased repression. It is in this context of political turmoil and mass uprisings that *Asinamali!* was created:

Out of the anger and passion of the residents of the Lamontville township
came the leader Msizi Dube. Passionately demonstrating against
proposed rent increases, he led the masses with the cry 'Asinamali!' – 'We
have no money!' This rallying phrase provided a focus for the
disenfranchised as well as a poignant description of the conditions of
Blacks throughout South Africa. (Ndlovu, 1986: 179).

Asinamali! was first performed at the Market Theatre[5] in 1985. The
play is set in a South African gaol. The five black male protagonists
recount their personal stories through word, song and dance, describing
the events that brought them to Durban Central Prison. Bongani is a
migrant labourer who has killed his girlfriend; Thami is a farm labourer
who was seduced by his white employer's wife and convicted under the
Immorality Act; Bhoyi is an activist who worked with Msizi Dube;
Solomzi is a petty gangster who pickpockets at mass funerals and
demonstrations; Bheki is unfairly convicted of political crimes after a
police raid on the house of his common-law wife and her activist son.

Us and them: black and white

A burst of sound and energy opens the play: five black men chant a
rhythmic song in Zulu. The men chant and sway in unison, establishing
a powerful visual and auditory image of collectivity. Their sense of
brotherhood is sustained throughout the play. They share a home (the
prison cell) where they eat, sleep and wash together; they are dressed in
identical khaki uniforms; and they are subject to the will of the same
authority figures (the prison warders). They are brothers in a hostile
world.

The opening song is interrupted by Bheki who jumps up to deliver
the first testimony of the play:

> I come from Zululand. I got a place to stay in Lamontville township, near
> the white city of Durban. During that time this man (*he points to his
> T-shirt which has the picture of a man*) Msizi Dube, a very strong leader
> and a powerful voice for our people, was killed. They killed him. The
> government spies killed him. The reason for his death was that he
> maintained that we have no money. A-SI-NA-MA-LI! so we cannot afford
> to pay the government's high rent increase. People took up this call:
>   'AAASSSIIINNNAAA MMMAAALLLIII!' and the police went to
> work. Many of us died and many of us went to jail, and it is still happening
> now. (Ngema, 1986: 182)

Bheki's speech serves, on one level, as the linguistic equivalent of the
opening image. His personal 'I' is subsumed by the collective 'we'
(1986: 192) so that his character acquires a communal identity. This
raises an immediate question, one that is asked and answered throughout the course of the play: who belongs to the collective 'we', to the
family, and who belongs to the implied other category, 'you'?

COURTESY OF THE MARKET THEATRE

Most pertinent to this and to my analysis of the play's actor-audience relationships is the antinaturalist style that *Asinamali!* adopts in relation to its audience. In the theatre there is no aesthetic closure around the text, separating it from its conditions of performance. In *Asinamali!* this is particularly germane – the audience is a protagonist, an important element in the production of meaning. The play is not an hermetic world into which the audience voyeuristically peeps; the actors draw the audience into the world of the play. When one of the characters re-enacts his life story, he is addressing both the on-stage audience (the four interlocutors) and its extension – the audience in the auditorium. The audience on stage guides the responses of the audience proper. The actors often address the audience directly, particularly when they break the narrative with song. At no point does the play slip into the naturalist mode of pretending that there is no audience, that the action is a slice of life. The actors tell stories within the story and the play delights in its own theatricality. In this context 'we' and 'you' is addressed to the audience. In using these words, the actor is defining an identity for the audience who, in turn, will place themselves in one of the two categories according to their extra-theatrical experiences.

Although the play was created by black South Africans under the direction of Mbongeni Ngema, it was controlled economically by the Market Theatre. *Asinamali!*'s commercial première was at the Market Theatre after having been performed in the townships around the

Zululand area. Hence the play must have anticipated a multiracial audience from the outset. Yvonne Banning notes that, unlike a play like *Sophiatown, Asinamali!* does not 'overtly present itself as a bridge across the gap between black and white "structures of feeling" [Raymond Williams' phrase]', but rather that 'many of its internal contradictions seem to arise because it recognises and enacts the gap that exists between white and black perceptions of socio-political conditions operating in South Africa.' (1989: 189).

Asinamali! constitutes two distinct and separate racial groups through the use of various linguistic and dramatic devices. Given that Zulu is understood almost exclusively by African audience members, the most apparent of these devices is the retreat into the 'linguistic privacy' (Banning's phrase) of Zulu at strategic moments of the play. The songs that punctuate the narrative are the most notable example, all of which are sung in Zulu and not translated into English (the lingua franca of the play). It is worth noting that the songs are almost all politically militant and often sexually explicit.

Although the play is multilingual, the various languages are not used interchangeably or as substitutes for one another. Rather, each language is imbued with political and racial meaning. Afrikaans is constituted as the language of the oppressor – most of the officials of the state machinery represented in the play speak in Afrikaans (among other languages). The use of English is more ambivalent. At times it is constituted as the other official language of the state (for example in the 'pipi office' and court scenes), and at times it is used as a substitute for Zulu (presumably to accommodate Market Theatre audiences). Despite this, Zulu is situated in opposition to English and Afrikaans: the language of the people is set up against the language of the state.

The court scene, in which Bheki is unfairly condemned to seven years in prison for political crimes, provides an arena in which the battle of languages can play itself out. The judge speaks in Afrikaans, the interpreter translates into English for Bheki who, in turn, speaks mostly in Zulu. The onslaught of the judge's words, doubled in quantity by the translator, overwhelms the accused and the audience.

> As meaning vanishes the sheer quantity of official words effectively crushes any verbal resistance and traps the victim into incomprehension and silence. Zulu and its speakers can only exist in the gaps and silences of official discourse. (Banning, 1989: 204)

The misunderstanding and confusion that arises from the rapid interchange of the three languages, as well as the humour that is derived from overliteral or mistranslation is best appreciated by those audience members who are trilingual. While the accused is rendered weak by his inability to understand Afrikaans and the subsequent barrage of words, these power relations are turned on their head for the audience members. Those who understand Zulu in addition to English and Afrikaans become a privileged section of the audience, united in their laughter at the slippages that occur between Zulu on the one hand and the two official languages on the other. For example, the court attempts to establish Bheki's guilt by proving that he is the father of Johannes Zulu, a political activist who has been convicted of attempting to burn the house of Mr Gasa, the councillor who informed on Msizi Dube. The dialogue runs as follows:

THAMI (*judge*): Is dit nie omdat Mnr Gasa vir Johannes Zulu hegtenis geneem het . . . nie?
BHOYI (*interpreter*): Was it not because Mr Gasa arrested Johannes Zulu . . .?
BHEKI (*accused*): Yes!
THAMI: Wat jou seun is?
BHOYI: Who is your son?
BONGANI (*court orderly, to the accused*): Lalela inkantolo. [Listen to the court.]
THAMI: Se hy nie papa na jou nie?
BHOYI: Does he not say 'papa' to you?
BHEKI: He is my son, yes, Kodwa akuyena owesende. [But he is not my blood son.]
BONGANI: Aha!
BHOYI: He does, your worship. (Ngema, 1986: 186)

The judge can understand only the first part of Bheki's answer, that 'he is my son', and the interpreter deliberately omits to translate Bheki's qualification. Only trilingual members of the audience can comprehend the crucial nuance. Moreover, this section of the audience alone can appreciate the power that the interpreter is afforded: the judgement of the court rests on the words of this petty official. Zulu language speakers – both in the character of the interpreter and the Zulu-speaking audience members – are advantaged in this moment. Thus Ngema deftly reverses traditional power relations: those officially disem-powered with regard to language enjoy a better understanding of the events.

The specific nature of the 'we' category is refined through the course of the play as the details of the lives of the five central characters accumulates. This is the category of people who suffer a litany of hardships which the various characters lament over and over again: life in the townships, rent increases, the humiliation of 'bloody fucking passbooks', work permits and v.d. offices, endless job-seeking, disen-franchisement. In other words, this is the category of black, particularly working-class, South Africans.

Racial polarization reaches a charged and confrontational climax when Bhoyi, after lambasting the audience with a tirade of 'the problems of the whole of South Africa', points to a white member of the audience, shouting, 'What is it? Hey! What is it? You, stand up. Hey mthatheni Bafana! [Go for him boys]' (Ngema, 1986: 212).

Us and them: men and women

The issues of black oppression and resistance are at the heart of
Asinamali!. Issues of sexual oppression and the problems and aspirations specific to women are not part of the subject matter of the play.
The gender ideology of the play is perhaps easily eclipsed by the forceful
enactment of racial and class struggle. But gender is strongly present in
the languages of race and class in *Asinamali!*. The racial categories that
the play constructs are gendered: the 'we' category excludes not only
whites, but black women too.

Women in *Asinamali!* hold four seemingly contradictory positions:
they are dependents; they are the objects of men who must be possessed
for the economic or political gains that they bring; they are mothers to be
exalted or despised for the children they produce; and they are a force of
chaos and destruction.

French theories of femininity, using Derridian deconstruction and
Lacanian psychoanalysis, can perhaps best explain how women can be
seen to be playing these conflicting roles simultaneously, with no
perceived contradiction. Hélène Cixous argues that the phallogocentric
system of Western metaphysics is structured by a set of hierarchical and
binary oppositions. The man/woman opposition, she argues, underlies a
series of oppositions: subject/object; activity/passivity; culture/nature;
father/mother; head/emotions; law/chaos, etc. A unified male identity is
constructed in the act of relegating femininity to the negative pole of the
binary opposition – male identity is the negative mirror image of female
identity. Cixous argues that the consequence of this 'death-dealing
binary thought' is that femininity is equated with passivity or death,
leaving no positive space for women. (Cixous in Jefferson and Robey,
1986: 210)

Picking up from Cixous, Julia Kristeva argues that if patriarchy
sees women as occupying a marginal position within the symbolic order,
then it can construe them as the limit or borderline of that order. Women
will then come to represent the necessary frontier between man and
chaos, but because of their marginality they will also always seem to
recede into and merge with the chaos of the outside. Because the
borderline is both the shield from the chaotic wilderness and part of it,
male culture can simultaneously venerate women as virginal mothers of
god, and vilify them as whores or Lilith figures.[6]

Women as dependents

Asinamali! distinguishes, along archetypal gender lines, those who
interact in the public arena from those confined to the private space of
the home. Seeking employment (or alternatively earning a living
through gangsterism) and engaging in political activity are established
as the domain of males in the dramatic world of the play.

The three activities are integrally linked. The 'Asinamali Campaign' that Msizi Dube launches is a protest against rent increases that
an impoverished and largely unemployed community cannot afford –

that poverty and politics are inextricable issues is something that 'the whole township understood' (Ngema, 1986: 215). Solomzi joins Bra Tony in his petty gangsterism as a means of earning money. Work and theft are almost interchangeable on this level in *Asinamali!*. Politics and gangsterism also become associated activities. If there are two heroes in the play, then they are Msizi Dube, the political activist, and Bra Tony, the gangster. Both are valorized by the men for their courage and audacity in the face of the police. Both are a thorn in the side of the state and its various apparatus. Both are 'big names' who receive newspaper coverage and have police files. And significantly, both are murdered (and martyred) by the state. Dube is assassinated and Bra Tony is shot by troops who invade Sebokeng during a mass funeral. It would seem that the play equates political and petty criminal activity in as much as they both constitute a defiance of the laws of the state.

The three associated activities are pursued exclusively by men. Msizi Dube is 'Awu i' nsizwa amakhosi [a man among men]' (Ngema, 1986: 211) – the men who participate in political protest action. That politics is a masculine domain is corroborated by the play's numerous freedom songs that make reference to the 'boys' or the 'guys' involved in the struggle.

Gangsterism too is a world of machismo, a world in which 'good men' like Bra Tony are valorized for stealing money hidden in women's panties. The act of sexual violation is as praiseworthy as the act of theft. In fact, theft itself is a triumph of manly bravura. Bheki relates a story in which three gangsters threw him a handbag they had just snatched from a woman. The gangsters had tricked him, for looking up, he realized that he was face-to-face with 'two Big Afrikaaner policemen'.

> And I said: Zinja [dogs] come! Don't run away. You've touched me. This is the day. How can you touch a lion? How can you touch a tiger? Here is the source of power! (*grabbing his genital area*) How can you touch me? (*he starts singing his praises in Zulu*)
>
> *All the prisoners jump up and go towards him and also sing his praises. They almost lift him from the floor as they shout his praises.* (Ngema, 1986: 200)

Bheki becomes the prisoners' deity of masculinity for demonstrating that his sexual potency is superior to that of the police. A smart thief is a virile thief.

Employment, the third thread in the nexus of public activity represented in the play, is desperately sought by the men to meet the needs of wives and children at home. The men share the burden of bread-winning. Part of this burden is the demeaning process of seeking employment. The most offensive of the bureaucracies involved in the issuing of work permits is the v.d. office. Bongani explains that until he came to Johannesburg, no one except his 'older wife' had 'seen his man'. But after one day in the big city, 'a white boy commanded me to open my fly and show him my man' (Ngema 1986: 207). The humiliation suffered in the 'pipi office' is metonymic for the experiences of job-hunting, subsequent employment by abusive bosses, and frequent interaction with the web of intransigent state bureaucracies: it insults one's 'manhood'.

Women remain in the private sphere of the home. There they become a burden to the men. They interfere with the lives the men lead in the public arena. The first reference to a woman in *Asinamali!* is to 'a girlfriend, a bitch' – Bongani's girlfriend whom he killed after she strangled their baby because 'there was no money to support [it]' (Ngema, 1986: 185). Bongani's words reveal the men's perception of women's identity: women are girlfriends, wives or mothers. What's more, the two categories of women – girlfriend and bitch – are identical to each other, synonymous, for Bongani, and the play never challenges his perception. Moreover, that Bongani has no sympathy for a woman who feels compelled to kill her child because she is poverty-stricken is the dominant sensibility in the world of the play. 'Bitch' is a resonant term of abuse in *Asinamali!*. One of the most despised characters of whom the men speak is Sergeant Schoeman, the warder who forces female prisoners to have sexual intercourse with him. In a moment of great anger, Bheki describes Schoeman as a 'bitch', confirming that a term of abuse traditionally reserved for women is the worst insult that can be evoked.

Women as political and economic weapons

Banning incisively articulates the role women play in *Asinamali!* as the providers of the means of economic and political power in a male struggle:

> Bheki's woman pays the train fares and her house in Lamontville enables him to become a 'boss in a dead man's home'. . . . The women prisoners are the means by which the Sergeant can find his own sexual gratification and demonstrate his power over the male prisoners. His sexual abuse of 'their' women enacts his abuse of his officially sanctioned power over them.
> Their sexual deprivation exemplifies their political impotence (1989: 210).

Similarly, Thami's highest pleasure in his sexual relationship with Mrs Van Niekerk lies in the victory that it constitutes over his racial and class enemy – Mr Van Niekerk. Solomzi relates a story to his fellow prisoners, the subtext of which literally identifies female sexuality with money. In his story, Solomzi and his gangster friend, Bra Tony, meet an (unnamed) Indian woman at Verulem Station. Since she is 'very pretty', Solomzi starts to talk to her. Bra Tony, however, interrupts his friend's seduction attempt in order to rob the woman of her money:

> 'Give me your panties' [Bra Tony demands of the woman]. She said: 'I'm having my period.' 'My baby, my sweetheart, give it to me.' You know

what she did? She pulled down her panties and Bra Tony grabbed the whole thing. A big roll of money came out man. (Ngema, 1986: 214–5)

Women as mothers

Women's procreative power is also seen as a weapon in male struggle. When the prisoners enact a political demonstration, they chant a song that pays tribute to Mrs Mandela, the mother of 'heroes', and vilifies Mrs Botha, the breeder of 'dogs' and 'armoured cars'. Neither woman is seen to play an active role in the struggle, a role in her own right. Their identities are simply that of mothers, and they are revered or despised for the offspring they produce.

> Sexual activity is thus an unacknowledged weapon in the economic and political struggle. But the weapon is women and the wielders of the weapon are men. (Banning, 1989: 210)

Women as the force of darkness

In the world of the play women are dangerous. Their sexuality is anarchic and destructive. It causes men to be imprisoned. And prison, according to the song of the inmates, is a place of death:

> Buti omuhle sewuzawufela ejele;
> Sewuzafela ejele butu omuhle
> mina nawe siboshwa sofela la.
> [A handsome guy will die in jail.
> Go on, you'll die in jail. Me and you
> prisoner, we'll die here.] (Ngema, 1986: 1930)

Of the five prisoners in the play, three are in gaol as the result of a woman. Bheki is imprisoned because he is mistakenly identified as the father of his common-law wife's activist son after police find Bheki 'sleeping on top of a woman who you claim is your wife' (Ngema, 1986: 185).

Bongani, the stutterer, gives this explanation for his imprisonment:

> Yeah! I got a girlfriend, a bitch. She fell pregnant. But there was no money to support the child. So she strangled the child in the toilet. I killed her too. And that's why I . . . I . . . I . . . (*motions with his hand to indicate that he wants to say I am here in prison*). (Ngema, 1986: 183)

Thami's story of his offence runs as follows:

> I come from the Afrikaaner farm in Bloemfontein, Orange Free State. Me and my white boss' wife, Mrs Van Niekerk . . . heh, heh (*indicates that they were making love*). Ya, and she liked it. (183)

These three women (like all the women in *Asinamali!*) have no physical presence on a stage occupied exclusively by men. They exist on the periphery of the dramatic world as the forces of darkness. Female sexuality threatens to erupt from the subtext and burst in from the margins of the play. The absence of women from the stage points to the play's perception of a sexual danger inherent in the female gender.

In attempting to account for women's historical absence from the stage, Sue-Ellen Case argues that by the late Middle Ages, the Church had secured the notion that immoral sexual conduct was the province of women. If the female body had become the site for sexuality, then women's performance in the public arena would elicit immoral responses from men, bringing disorder to the social body. (Case, 1988: 20) Women were consequently banned from the stage. Although by the time of Shakespeare's plays the theatre was no longer a Church-supported institution, the nature of its religious roots was still evident, if substantially transformed. The best way to alleviate the danger implicit in the female body was for males to assimilate female roles.[7]

Asinamali! appears to subscribe to this view. For most of the play, women are safely confined to the off-stage margins. One scene employs the dramatic technique of gender-substitute performance. Thami's re-enactment of Mrs Van Niekerk is reminiscent of pantomime in which men use caricatured gesture, movement and intonation and a falsetto voice to signal to the audience that a woman is being depicted. Even this momentary whisper from the female gender is carefully controlled by the play. As Banning points out, 'this encounter . . . is tightly constrained by male discourse to marginalise and diminish it' (1989: 211). The stereotypical and hyperbolic responses of the male audience on the stage guide the audience in their responses. That Thami has secured his sexual 'daily bread' is a fine accomplishment in the eyes of the interlocutors, that the provider of his daily bread is white and the boss's wife is cause for great laughter, hooting, cheering and gestures of amazement and awe.

This type of male assimilation of female roles is a visual demonstration of the distinction to be made between 'Woman' as a male-produced fiction and historical women. Thami's vocabulary of female gesture and intonation consists quite clearly of male-originated signs. The notion and depiction of women in *Asinamali!* is, I have argued, derived entirely from a male point of view. And while I am not suggesting that the perspective of the gendered opposite is necessarily 'inauthentic', in the case of *Asinamali!* I would argue that the male portrayal of female characters is likely to remain alien to many female members of the audience. That speculation aside, the perception of female sexuality that the play presents places women firmly in a category that is other, burdensome and dangerous to men. Women are to be found on the shadowy margins of the play, in the silent negative pole of the binary opposition, outside of the 'we' and pushed into the 'you'. Women are part of the category that stands in opposition to the five central characters and the ever-diminishing section of the audience that shares their experiences.

The collectivity of the men is accentuated by the stylistic and visual qualities of the play.

The gender of form

The bond of brotherhood and shared experience is accentuated by the stylistic qualities of the play. The language of the actors is partially sung, partially chanted, and is almost rhymed; they dance and gyrate with a beauty and a frenzied energy and create a compelling aesthetic of sweat. Much of the language, sound and song takes the form of choral verse. The actors chant lines together; one voice shouts out a slogan and the other four respond; one actor speaks while the others sing or hum in the background; they sing most of the songs collectively; and when telling a story they create a barrage of voices that rapidly succeed one another so that it is difficult to distinguish which actor's voice is being heard and whose story is being told. The five bodies and voices merge into one creating the effect of a collective being and a collective experience of suffering, anger, amusement and resistance.

The unity of the group is reinforced on a visual level. The actors are often situated in a row in which they rock, sway and dance in unison. Repetition of action is also used to enhance the sense of group experience. When one of the actors tells of the medical examination to which he was subjected during the process of obtaining a work permit, for example, the actors queue up and successively re-enact the ritual whereby the genitals are examined. This leads to a visual representation of the strong emotional connexion between the players. When Solomzi is mourning over the recollected death of his friend Bra Tony, for example, the others mourn with him, sharing and expressing in song and movement his own pain. Similarly when one man is celebrating a joyous memory, the others jump up and down and hug each other like little boys sharing a moment of delight. Stylistically and visually, women stand outside of the collective, the enmeshed team of brothers fighting a hostile world.

Conclusion

The battle of the sexes plays itself out within and beneath the struggle for racial and class liberation in *Asinamali!*. Class, race and gender meanings reciprocally constitute each other. It is a sad irony that the discourses of the gaolers and the gaoled – the oppressors and the oppressed – converge on one major issue: women. For both camps, women must be contained and marginalized. *Asinamali!*, in failing to consider gender ideology, reinforces the dominant ideology which deems women a threat to the most fundamental order – the rudimentary social matrix, civilization itself, that which makes the social possible. Female sexuality embodies chaos and danger; their primary usefulness is in the political or economic power they can afford to men. Thus the resistance discourse of the prisoners reinforces, in crucial respects, the dominant discourse it despises.

Msizi Dube's political leadership and violent death inspired, in the words of the preface to the play:

> a group of 'committed artists' whose primary goal was the revelation and ultimate eradication of racial and social inequality in South Africa. Out of this concern Mbongeni Ngema's *Asinamali!* was born. (Ngema, 1986: 179).

The process of revelation or education is primarily directed at those who do not suffer the inequality – the 'them' category. The 'we' category, on the other hand, is called to action, to understand and eradicate their oppression. In constructing the 'we' category, *Asinamali!* binds a section of the audience into an ideological unity. The sheer energy of the players pushes the dramatic world on to the edges of the world outside the play, urging its brothers in the audience to act now. 'Go for him boys.' But what of the women, those who suffer the inequalities that the play represents, and more? They are excluded from the brotherhood of freedom fighters who are bound together by their struggle against apartheid, and swept up by the mobilizatory force of the play. The gender ideology of *Asinamali!* undermines its primary imperative.

Notes

Carol Steinberg is a lecturer in the Department of Dramatic Art, University of the Witwatersrand, Johannesburg. She is an executive member of the Performing Arts Workers Equity (PAWE), a nonracial organization committed to the education of theatre workers and to the improvement of their conditions of work.

The photographs are of different casts of *Asinamali!*

1 See Steadman (1990) for a more detailed categorization of anti-apartheid theatre.
2 I am referring to Albie Sachs's paper 'Preparing Ourselves for Freedom' which can be found in de Kok and Press (1990).
3 Mbongeni Ngema is a leading black South African playwright, director and producer. His company, Committed Artists, created the musicals *Sarafina* and *Township Fever*, which have both received international acclaim.
4 An analysis of the political implications of the play's racial categorization lies outside of the scope of this paper.
5 The Market Theatre, established in 1976, is the key institution in South Africa that provided the material conditions for local, often anti-apartheid, companies to produce their work at a time when state repression was often severe.
6 See Jefferson and Robey (1986: 209–21).
7 For a detailed version of this argument see Case (1988: 5–28).

References

BANNING, Y. (1989) 'English Language Usage in South African Theatre Since 1976' unpublished Masters thesis.
BARRETT, M. (1984) *Women's Oppression Today* London: Verso.
CASE, S. (1988) *Feminism and Theatre* London: Macmillan.
DE KOK, I. and PRESS, K. (1990) *Spring is Rebellious* Cape Town: Bachu Books.
GREENE, G. and KAHN, C. (1985) editors, *Making a Difference* London and New York: Methuen.
JEFFERSON, A. and ROBEY, D. (1986) *Modern Literary Theory: A Comparative Introduction* London: Batsford.
NDLOVU, D. (1986) *Woza Afrika!* New York: George Braziller.
NEWTON, J. and ROSENFELT, D. (1985) editors, *Feminist Criticism and Social Change* New York and London: Methuen.
NGEMA, M. (1986) '*Asinamali!*' in NDLOVU (1986).
STEADMAN, I. (1990) 'Theatre Beyond Apartheid' unpublished inaugural lecture.
WEEDON, C. (1988) *Feminist Practice and Poststructuralist Theory* Oxford and New York: Basil Blackwell.

IBU OR THE BEAST: Gender Interests in Two Indonesian Women's Organizations[1]

Saskia Wieringa

Introduction

One of the most stimulating attempts to develop a theoretical frame-work for the analysis of women's organizations is that of Maxine Molyneux, who makes the distinction between organization for practical and strategic gender interests. Part of the attraction of the distinction is that it promises to be a tool in efforts to assess the performance of women's organizations. However, these concepts are widely, and generally uncritically, used in discussions which deal with 'women and development' issues, particularly in relation to women's organizations in the South. I have various analytical and conceptual problems with the concepts of practical and strategic gender interests. In the space of this article, I will not be able to spell these out in detail. Instead I will use the example of two mass organizations of Indonesian women to focus on some of the ambiguities in these concepts.

Molyneux has suggested that it might be useful to differentiate between women's strategic and women's practical gender interests in assessing the 'success' of certain policies regarding women, specifically addressing the performance of the socialist state of Nicaragua. Strategic gender interests she defines as being 'derived from the analysis of women's subordination and from the formulation of an alternative, more satisfactory set of arrangements to those which exist'. Practical gender interests, on the other hand, 'are generally a response to an immediate perceived need and they do not generally entail a strategic goal such as women's emancipation or gender equality' (Molyneux, 1985: 240).

I will address myself here to the conceptualization of the term 'practical gender interests'. I will argue that the critical distinction in assessing the performance of, in this case two organizations, lies not so much in the nature of the activities they carry out, or in the issues which their programmes address, but rather in the underlying perspective which determines the way these activities or programmes are shaped. In this discussion I will focus on both the continuities and the dissimilarities in the activities of the two organizations under discussion and in the perspectives from which they work/ed.

The organizations we will deal with are the Gerwani (Indonesian Women's Movement) and the PKK (Family Welfare Guidance). There are wide differences between these two women's mass organizations. Gerwani was the left-wing women's organization in Indonesia which was banned after the coup of 1965. Many thousands of its members were brutally killed in the ensuing campaign to wipe out all traces of the former prominent left organizations, and especially of the PKI, the Indonesian communist party. The army under General Suharto succeeded in exploiting the latent fear of the 'Communist Beast' to portray Gerwani members as morally depraved women. PKK is the present-day mass organization set up by Indonesia's New Order government. Although the government presents it emphatically as a general mass organization dealing with family affairs it is generally seen as a women's organization. Women are supposed to play a prominent role in the family so in practice the PKK is almost entirely directed towards women.

Using Molyneux's terminology, both Gerwani and PKK can be seen to address primarily women's practical gender interests. However, I will show that underlying strategic concerns informed the practice of these organizations in such a way that, although they carry out comparable activities, the effects of their work has fundamentally different implications. I will start with giving some historical background.

Indonesia since 1950

After a prolonged war of liberation against the Dutch colonial power, Indonesia gained its independence in 1949. Ir Sukarno was the first president. He had actively tried to engage the support of the Indonesian women's movement in the national struggle. And indeed women had come to the fore: they had set up public kitchens, organized medical help for the wounded, and had been active in establishing communications between the various guerrilla groups; some women had also fought in the guerrilla forces. In the new Constitution women were granted the same legal and political rights as men, although the marriage law was not reformed, an issue the women's organizations had been fighting for long before the Second World War.

The unity of the women's organizations achieved during the revolutionary years soon crumbled (Wieringa, 1985). In the face of the coming elections (1955) women started organizing themselves along the various political streams. Apart from this political diversification, women's organizations based on religious and ethnic differences came up as well.

From 1950 until 1959 Indonesia knew an unstable system of parliamentary democracy. The elections in 1955, the first and only really democratic elections in Indonesia so far, did not bring the desired stability. The Communist Party of Indonesia, the PKI, surprisingly gained a strong fourth position in the elections, with 16.3 per cent of the votes. Gradually, the Indonesian political scene became dominated by tensions between the three dominant political groups, the army, the Muslims[2] and the Communists. President Sukarno's personal charisma was the main mediating factor in preserving a delicate balance. He became increasingly frustrated in his efforts to forge national unity, and in 1957 he created a National Council in which all non-party-affiliated functional groups participated, including the army. In the following years this Council, chaired by Sukarno himself, became the major locus of political power (Feith, 1962; May, 1978; Ricklefs, 1981).

In 1959 Sukarno swept aside parliament and declared the policy of Guided Democracy. In 1960 he launched the Nasakom formula: Nationalist (NAS), religious (A from *agama*, religion) and Communist (KOM) forces should cooperate to build a stable and prosperous Indonesia. For the first time the Communists were drawn into the government, much to the dislike of the army, which, although officially left out of Nasakom, increasingly began to dominate the political, economic and of course military scene. Sukarno needed both the PKI and the army in his struggle against the conservative forces in society. The PKI because they were able to supply him with the mass support he wanted, and the army because it supported him in his nationalist, military campaigns. Increasingly, Sukarno sought to build national unity through mass military campaigns: the struggle for the liberation of Irian Jaya and the Anti-Malaysia campaign.[3]

Although the attention of the president was turned towards the struggle against imperialism more than towards the construction of domestic socialism, some socialist measures were introduced, such as a land reform in 1960. When little progress was made in the implementation of this law, the left-wing farmers' union, supported by the PKI and Gerwani, started their 'one-sided actions': peasants tried to acquire land by force. Around 1964 this policy led to enormous tensions in the countryside: conservative landholders, many of them belonging to Islamic groups, became antagonized.

In this extremely delicate political situation, with an almost bankrupt economy, on 30 September 1965, a group of middle-ranking army men abducted and killed six conservative generals. They tried to get the support of the PKI and of President Sukarno, but how far they were actually involved in this clumsy *putsch* remains unclear (Anderson, 1987; Gunawan, 1968; May, 1978; Mortimer, 1974; Törnquist, 1984; Wertheim, 1978 and 1985). There are also indications that the current president, Suharto, was involved, but there is no clear proof of his involvement either (Wertheim, 1985). However, General Suharto quickly regained control. He managed to instigate a mass campaign in which the full blame for the coup was laid on the PKI. In the following months the PKI and the country's left-wing mass organizations, including the Gerwani, were completely destroyed. Most reports agree that around half a million people were killed. Tens of thousands were imprisoned, of whom only some two hundred were ever tried.

In 1968, Suharto became the country's new president. The army and the civil services were purged of people with leftist or left nationalist sympathies, a process which is still continuing. The army has gained absolute dominance in political and civilian matters; even the Muslim groups which had assisted the army greatly in the mass murders of left people are left with less power than they had before 1965. All mass organizations including the women's organizations were put under strict government control. PKK is one of the government's instruments to propagate its policies among women.

In comparing Gerwani and PKK I will start by discussing their position in the national political arena. I will then focus on the structure of the organizations, the range of their activities and their ideology.

Position in the national-political arena

Gerwani grew in a process of nation-building. After the national liberation war Sukarno forged national unity by using a mixture of nationalist and socialist slogans and programmes. Many Gerwani leaders and members had been active in the war and the organization fully supported the struggle for a unified Indonesian republic. Sukarno himself had always insisted on the participation of women in the nationalist struggle (in fact, the subtitle of his book *Sarinah* is: *The Duty of Women in the Struggle for the Indonesian Republic*). Later his interest in women's issues dwindled. In 1960 he is quoted as saying: 'We don't need a feminist struggle. That time has passed. It is not the opposite sex that causes the inequalities in society' (*Harian Rakyat*, 18 May 1960).

Gerwani, however, did find some fault with the male sex and also with the president himself. While the majority of women's organizations was struggling for a marriage law in which polygamy would be prohibited, Sukarno's private life became filled with more and more wives. No more help in the struggle against polygamy could be expected from the 'Supreme Shepherd of the Women's Revolutionary Movement' as he had himself called. Unlike another prominent women's organization, Perwari,[4] however, Gerwani decided not to attack the president too harshly for this betrayal of the feminist cause which he had supported so heartily. Gerwani leaders suppressed their individually felt frustration about the conduct of Sukarno in the hope of the ultimate rewards of the 'just and prosperous society' which their polygamous president promised them (Wieringa, 1988a).

In justifying this political choice, the space for Gerwani's feminist politics was considerably narrowed down. Sukarno's 'betrayal' of the

SASKIA WIERINGA

Old time activist in the Nationalist Women's movement. Java.

feminist cause meant a weakening of the 'feminist' wing of Gerwani. Their support of the president meant that the gap with Perwari, formerly an ally, widened. Yet the cooperation with the PKI and Sukarno afforded the Gerwani leadership the opportunity to challenge women's subordinate position in new ways. It gave them a certain legitimacy to make feminist claims to the government. Also, it allowed the women's organization to publicly denounce the idea that women are submissive and docile, and to stress the militancy of Indonesian women. With the support of the PKI, Gerwani tried to convince the government of the urgency of two of its feminist concerns: the demands for a new marriage law and the demand that women should be allowed to be elected as village heads. Thus Gerwani's position, although circum-scribed by its ties to the PKI and the desire of the PKI to support Sukarno, nevertheless allowed it to stage various antigovernment demonstrations. The organization supported women workers and peasants against landlords and factory owners, and severely criticized the government's economic failures, concentrating on the issue of food prices.

It is difficult to assess how 'successful' Gerwani was in its lobbying. On a practical level their demands were not met. The new marriage law was not passed until 1974; it restricted polygamy but did not abolish it. The struggle to have women accepted as elected village leaders died down quietly; at present hardly anything is heard of it. Likewise their economic demands were not met; on the contrary, the economic decline of the country was disastrous. On an ideological level it is virtually impossible to find out to what measure the consciousness of Gerwani members was raised before 1965. It was most unsafe to refer to one's association with Gerwani after 1965.

The relationship between Gerwani and the PKI, a major actor in the national field, is complex. To an increasing extent, the women's organization supported many policies of the PKI, particularly in the international field. The PKI 'used' Gerwani to mediate its policies to a potential electorate among women. From the end of the fifties, Gerwani members were increasingly mobilized for mass rallies. On the local level, Gerwani members demonstrated against arrests of communist peasant or labour leaders. But Gerwani never supported the PKI automatically. Gerwani leadership frequently disapproved of the PKI line. On the whole, they resented the fact that the PKI leadership did not pay much attention to women's issues. Unlike Lenin and Mao for instance, PKI chairman Aidit rarely paid more than lip service to the 'woman question'. Over all, the PKI saw women's public role essentially as an extension of their domestic tasks. To the PKI the 'woman question' would be solved when the colonial, imperialist and feudal aspects of Indonesian society had been removed. Gerwani was more dubious about this and at any rate they wanted immediate changes. Women's double burden, which the PKI recognized as an issue to be resolved in a vague, distant future, impeded women presently, so Gerwani leaders said, and therefore kindergartens had to be set up and men had to share in the domestic work. For similar reasons they were of the opinion that the struggle for a democratic marriage law should not wait any longer. Male PKI members who wanted to marry a second wife were denounced as antirevolutionary, a strong accusation against a member of a Communist party.

Because PKK consists of the wives of civil servants and members of the armed forces, the link between the present government and the PKK is much more direct. PKK cadres are members of the government party, the Golkar (acronym of *Golongan Karya*, a collection of functional groupings). The government stimulates a capitalist path of development which is built on internal stability and order. This stability and order in its turn is forged in an incessant campaign against the supposed evils of communism.[5] Ideologically, therefore, PKK is set up to construct an image of womanhood which is virtually the opposite of the ideal of womanhood Gerwani tried to create. Not militance, but obedience is stressed. Women are called upon to sacrifice themselves in the interests of a male-dominated household, which, as the 'smallest unit of society' is ultimately designed to support government politics. The full weight of the state machinery is used to create obedient wives and submissive supporters of the central government. If individual PKK leaders disagree with either the hierarchical line of command or with the content of the programmes they are supposed to carry out, their concerns cannot be translated into open debates and dissent. The only way in which they can show their discontent is by becoming passive. They cannot constructively try to mediate the interests of PKK members to the government if those interests are not parallel to those of the government. Although officially PKK cadres are 'volunteers', in actual practice they are virtually unpaid government servants. They are supposed to serve their government so faithfully that their interests practically converge with government interests.

Structure

The internal structure of Gerwani and PKK is characterized by both parallels and dissimilarities. Neither Gerwani nor the PKK were autonomous organizations in the sense that many present-day feminist organizations are (Wieringa, 1988b). PKK is the government women's wing, while Gerwani was firmly entrenched in the 'left family', although the organization never became officially affiliated to the PKI.

Another parallel was the mass base of both organizations. Both sought to organize the masses of women but from a different perspective: PKK to subordinate women, Gerwani to make women critical members of society, supporting a leftist political position. Also, both organizations had hierarchical structures. But the hierarchy in each organization operated in different ways. The PKK does not even make an attempt to feign a democratic face. Orders come from above and have to be carried out.

The structure of Gerwani was democratic centralist. This meant that the voices from above were heard more loudly than voices from below. Yet, especially on the various congresses held, common members could and did express their views and communicated their concerns to the leadership. The Gerwani leadership in its turn tried to intervene on behalf of its members on the national scene.

Gerwani's leadership was mainly middle class. This is common among most mass-based organizations operating on national level. The women achieved their leadership positions by their personal capacities, hard work and their interest in study. Although many leaders had more or less close ties with male leaders of the PKI, in no way was their position derived from their husbands. There were quite a few cases in which women had a higher position than their husbands. They were not a homogeneous group of women and had sometimes fierce debates among themselves. Historically, a shift in their allegiance can be noted: from the end of the fifties onwards they moved closer to the PKI.

The leaders of the PKK are both upper-class political women and men and middle-class women and men. Although the women do the actual work, their husbands have important functions behind the scene: they are the theorists and 'guides'. The women leaders have all acquired their positions through marriages to top-level men. Thus their leadership is ascribed and is not necessarily related to any personal achievements, or even to an interest in the PKK. This situation often leads to cases of mismanagement, passivity and unconcern. On the other hand, capable women whose husbands are too low in the government hierarchy to 'offer' their wives a high position in the PKK may also become frustrated: their capacities are underutilized, there is no place for their enthusiasm, drive and critical insights in the decision-making process.

As the government structure reaches down to all layers of society and to all corners of the archipelago, PKK cadres are active all over Indonesia. Discontinuity in PKK's activities may occur when leaders have to withdraw because their husbands lose or step down from their influential positions. Within these constraints some women are able to find an outlet for their energies in the PKK and they may even try to make use of the possibilities which PKK offers them to do some meaningful work.

The major concern of PKK leaders is not the question of women's subordination in Indonesian society, but support of the government in power. The structure is centralist, hierarchical and authoritarian. PKK's major objective is to integrate Indonesian families in the development process. Issues like unequal power relations within families are not dealt with. No attention is paid to the voice of the common members of the PKK; only if certain targets are not reached does the PKK leadership try to address the obstacles which they distinguish. In those cases where capable cadres are able to carry out elements of the PKK programme which have a direct relevance to women's daily needs, the daily concerns of the members can be served.

As far as the composition of Gerwani's membership is concerned, until 1954 both members and leaders were mainly recruited from earlier women's organizations, groups which had been active during the war and from left-wing or nationalist parties. Throughout its history the leadership continued to be mainly recruited from these groups but the membership widened up. After 1954 the majority of the new members came from poor urban or peasant backgrounds with no clear organizational history. Also middle and lower-middle-class housewives joined the organization. Members were registered and paid dues. Apart from the reasons listed above to join Gerwani, women were probably largely drawn to the organization because of its social work. Women who dropped their children at the kindergarten were almost automatically registered as Gerwani members. Many women too were attracted to the organization because it offered them practical help and advice when they were unilaterally divorced or experienced other problems in their marriages. Others simply joined because members in their families belonged to other progressive mass organizations like the youth organization, the peasant or trade union, or because they wanted to avail themselves of the courses it offered. Gerwani activities on the local level were generally planned on the basis of the direct needs of the women, and after their problems had been discussed extensively.

PKK cadres draw the participants of their activities from roughly the same groups as Gerwani did. However, PKK cadres come to the women of the villages and *kampung* (neighbourhoods) with pre-established programmes. Women's concerns which do not fall within such programmes will not be taken into account. If members happen to live in an area in which the leaders are active and capable, they may profit from the organization. Provided PKK members do not question the government's wisdom, do not strive to transform the existing order and do not rebel against the ideal of wifehood which is propagated by the organization, they may find something in the organization for them. Members who are enthusiastic about the organization and who are capable and willing to fulfil a more responsible position within PKK cannot become cadres. They can not follow cadre courses, as Gerwani members could; the only way of upward mobility is through the career of their husbands. Thus the PKK programme does not take women's concerns nor women's rights as its starting point; rather women's duties as obedient wives and loyal citizens are stressed. The PKK leadership decides the priorities of the organization in line with government policy.

Range of activities

The greatest parallels between the two organizations can be found in the range of their activities. Both started from the direct economic needs of the women they work with, but they did so from a completely different perspective.

Gerwani members at the local level carried out manifold activities. They set up crèches, gave literacy classes and cooking and sewing lessons, helped women in their agricultural tasks and encouraged them to engage in non-farming income generating projects. Apart from this they also intervened on behalf of the women in conflicts with landlords or husbands.

Activities to be carried out were determined by meetings of the members themselves. Gerwani cadres acted in those meetings as careful listeners to the needs of the village women. In carrying out the plans made up at those meetings the effectiveness of the cadres was often circumscribed by the insufficient resources available.

PKK members also engage in a multitude of activities. They may, for instance, learn some practical skills, such as sewing or making cookies to sell. The skills taught are usually an extension of their domestic activities. If the PKK engages in small-scale income generating projects, these projects are not geared towards making women

SASKIA WIERINGA

Islamic Women's group with girls from the orphanage they sponsor. Bukittingi, Sumatera.

economically independent, as Gerwani tried to do, but to supplement the 'main' income of the husband. Not all of the activities of the PKK members deserve to be called directly relevant to their daily problems (eg. courses in arranging flowers, and beauty contests.)

The *Pancasila*[6] course is the first activity on PKK's list of 10 points. It is obligatory for the whole population, and it is routinely given to those PKK members who have not yet followed one. After that, the cadres are more free to select elements from the programme. However, in actual fact their choices are very much determined by the activities which are carried out through other government agencies (such as the departments of health, education and agriculture) and by the priorities set by the village co-operative, the LKMD (*Lembaga Ketahanan Masyarakat Desa*, Institute for Village Resilience). The village headman, husband of the chair of the PKK, is the head of this co-operative, which is the official organ through which the government programmes are carried out at the local level.

Ideology

The greatest difference between the two organizations is to be found in their ideological perspectives. The two organizations have completely different world views. Gerwani fought for a transformation of society, and for women to be active and vocal members of that society. The PKK wants to 'integrate' women into the present right-wing military bureaucratic state (Crouch, 1978), without questioning either the nature of that state or indeed the conditions under which women are already 'integrated'.

Each organization has upheld a different ideal of womanhood. Both have propagated 'ibuism', but what kind of *ibu*s (literally 'mothers') have they proposed? Neither organization sought to challenge women's roles as wife and mother. However, PKK's *ibu*s are obedient and loyal, don't protest, and submit themselves to the authority of husbands and fathers, and ultimately of *Bapak Pembangunan* (Father of Development), President Suharto, himself. Whereas Gerwani's women were independent and strong; they were not submissive, and they were often stimulated to follow the examples of strong warriorlike women like Srikandi (one of the characters in the *wayang*, the national shadow puppet theatre). Gerwani women were also actually trained to become guerrilla fighters. Also, Gerwani members were in the forefront of the struggle against sexual violence against women, such as wife-beating and rape. These are not issues that PKK is concerned with.

Because the gap between the popularly held image of Gerwani in present-day Indonesia, as morally depraved human beings, and the ideas Gerwani members themselves had about their own organization differ so vastly, it is interesting to examine Gerwani's ideology somewhat more closely. Due to limits of space, I will not be able to give more than an indication of Gerwani's ideas. Generally its ideology might be characterized as eclectic with a preponderance of socialist ideas. Elements from Indonesian history figured strongly in its teaching. An issue like the introduction of women into waged labour, a Marxist panacea to end women's oppression, did not gain much prominence, essentially because the issue was irrelevant for the lower-class women, who were all earning some income. Gerwani's socialism can be firmly located in the national ideological discourse of its time. Socialist inspiration was also drawn from the achievements of other socialist countries such as China or Russia, for instance in the field of child care or of socializing the household. Regularly articles appeared in both *Harian Rakyat* (the PKI newspaper) and in *Api Kartini* (a Gerwani periodical intended for middle-class women) about these issues. A topic which the Gerwani leadership introduced in the national arena was their opposition to the 'moral decadence' which they associated with the products of American imperialism, such as films.

Gerwani also paid attention to more traditional women's issues. Both in *Harian Rakyat* and in *Api Kartini* emphasis was put on women's roles as mothers and wives. Recipes, articles on dress-making and child care regularly appeared. Gerwani saw itself as carrying special responsibility for child care, much attention was paid to Children's Day. But whatever emphasis the organization put on women's roles as wives and mothers, Gerwani promoted women's roles as social activists as well. To the great dismay of Islamic and Christian groups, Gerwani members were stimulated to fight for their own rights and to join demonstrations against landlords and factory owners. Sometimes demonstrations against the state were held (as in the anti-price-rise

SASKIA WIERINGA

Ibu Salawati Daiud with some of her friends. Jakarta.

demonstrations), at other times women were mobilized to support national policies that the leadership approved of. The keyword which Gerwani consistently used in this respect is *gegigihan* (militance). The militant role of Gerwani members in Indonesia's 'continuous revolution' is stressed, both in the sense of defending that revolution against its 'imperialist' enemies and in struggles against landlords. High moral standards were set for cadres. Gerwani's chairperson Umi Sardjono listed in 1964 the following characteristics: 'Gerwani works diligently to create cadres who are courageous, capable, possess culture and who possess the following three good character traits: they can work well, they study well and they have good morals' (Sardjono, 1964: 4).

To conclude this section on Gerwani's ideology, it has to be emphasized that, contrary to what was said about Gerwani later, the organization upheld the ideal of women living in morally correct, heterosexual, monogamous families. In this way it did not differ much from the PKK. But there is a difference in the way Gerwani and PKK saw the family. Gerwani propagated families which would live according to both national and revolutionary norms. The relationship between wife and husband would be characterized by mutual aid and respect and equality, not by subordination. All members of those families would be involved in progressive organizations, but in their own right, and according to the capacities and energies of each. Also, the women's organization recognized that the double burden which women faced, as well as their marital problems, were not just the consequence of feudalism, but were rooted in the everyday conduct of individual women and men. On the whole women were seen as independent persons, in the social, economic and political field.

PKK conceptualizes families in a different way. A hierarchy between husband and wife is stressed. PKK promotes the *Panca Dharma Wanita* (Five Duties of Women), which are: to be loyal companions of their husbands, to procreate for the nation, to educate and guide their children, to regulate the household and, lastly, to be a useful member of society. All these tasks preferably are to be carried out in a way which is according to the *Kodrat Wanita* (Woman's Nature). This *Kodrat* entails that women are *lemah lembut* (soft and weak), don't speak out loudly, and certainly not in their own interests, don't push their own interests against those of husbands and fathers, but are instead compliant wives and mothers and dutiful daughters. Women's central role is seen to be located primarily in the family. Contrary to the Indonesian socio-economic reality, where poor women are generally major income earners (Wieringa, 1981), their economic role is largely denied. Women are essentially seen as appendages to their husbands, while it is 'the husband's function to bear responsibility for and protect the family, act as a responsible leader, give examples of good behaviour and earn a living for the family' (Moenadi, 1971: 5).

Concluding remarks

Coming back to my discussion on the distinction Molyneux made between women's practical and strategic gender interests, I must conclude that both Gerwani and PKK have carried out a similar range of activities based on the immediate perceived needs of women. However, both organizations have worked towards different goals. Politically Gerwani fought for a transformation of society in which women would be active and vocal members, whereas PKK wants to 'integrate' women into the present state. Moreover, there is a vital difference in the way the leaders of both organizations conceptualize womanhood.

Thus both Gerwani and PKK can be said to have engaged themselves mainly with what Molyneux calls 'practical gender interests'. But they have done so in different ways. Gerwani cadres tried to link women's practical, daily concerns to issues of national interest. In cooking lessons issues of landownership and imperialism might be discussed, in the literacy courses the president's book and speeches were studied. In this way members were given political education. This form of consciousness-raising received most attention in the years between the 1954 congress and the early sixties. After that period cadres were urged to enlist as many members as possible. With so much emphasis being put on the quantative growth of the organization, consciousness-raising was sometimes neglected.

Such discussions are absent from any cooking demonstration organized by the PKK I have witnessed. Generally the recipes are composed in Jakarta, which may mean that they require ingredients which are not locally available in every island or region. Cooking contests are regularly held in which the emphasis is put not so much on the nutritional value of the various dishes, but rather on the way in which they are presented.

Molyneux asserts that 'these practical gender interests do not in themselves challenge the prevailing forms of gender subordination, but they arise directly out of them.' (Molyneux, 1985: 241) In the light of the discussion presented here this position is not tenable. The major criterion to determine whether a concern with 'practical gender interests' challenges the gender relations in society is not the nature of those interests in themselves. Given their different perspectives on society and womanhood, the effects of PKK's and of Gerwani's concerns with the same type of activities have been quite different. In the case of the PKK the way the organization tackles the daily problems of women only serves to reinforce women's gender subordination by locating women's position firmly in the household under male leadership. Whereas Gerwani, while to a large part concentrating on the same problems, managed to gradually project such a different image of women that it greatly antagonized right-wing groups. So antagonized were they in fact that when grotesque accusations against Gerwani members appeared,[7] enough people used the excuse to kill Gerwani members in order to 'purge' society.

Thus, although both organizations have centred a large part of their activities around women's 'practical gender interests' they have done so in a critically different manner. From one point of view those observers who point out the continuity of the activities of both organizations are right. However, the PKK's involvement never constitutes a threat to the prevailing order; it even strengthens women's subordination. While Gerwani can be said to have threatened the existing social order and gender subordination. Although it may be true that it did not always attack the existing sex-gender system in as systematic and consistent a way as our present-day feminist theories may dictate, it is also true that its attacks were none the less so stinging that conservative, patriarchal forces were highly antagonized. As such it addressed issues that most present-day feminists would call 'strategic'. We might even come to the conclusion that the viciousness of the attacks against Gerwani and the extent of the murders not only point to the failure of the organization to bring about meaningful change, but also should be seen as the sad proof of the ineffectiveness of their rebellion against the forces oppressing women.

Notes

Saskia Wieringa is a lecturer in the Women and Development Programme at the Institute of Social Studies in The Hague, Holland. She did fieldwork in Indonesia, India and Peru, made a documentary film on batik labourers, wrote a novel and published widely on issues of women and organization. She is currently editing a book on Women's Movements in Historical Perspective.

Abbreviations used in this article:
AK – Api Kartini
Gerwani – Gerakan Wanita Indonesia
Golkar – Golongan Karya.
HR – Harian Rakyat
Nasakom – Nasionalis, Agama, Komunis
PKK – Pembinaan Kesejahteraan Keluarga
PKI – Partai Komunis Indonesia
Perwari – Persatuan Wanita Republik Indonesia

1 An extended version of this article will appear in: *Stretching Boundaries: Women's Movements and Organizations in Historical Perspective*, ed. S. Wieringa, forthcoming.
2 Indonesia has the largest Islamic population of the world. Generally they are divided into two groups, the *santri* who we might nowadays call the fundamentalists, and the *abangan*, the majority of the Islamic population, who mix their Islamic faith with many elements from the traditional Indonesian religions and/or with Hinduism. When I here refer to the Muslim groups, I refer to political organizations mainly made up of *santris*. The other two political actors addressed in this article, the PKI and the army, also contain many Muslims, but they are mostly *abangan*.
3 Since 1959 Indonesia claimed sovereignty over Irian Jaya, the last remaining part of the archipelago under Dutch control. In December 1961 the conflict turned into an armed confrontation. On 1 May 1963 Irian Jaya was placed under direct Indonesian rule, on condition that in 1969 a plebiscite would be held for the Papuan population. In September 1963 Indonesia embarked on a confrontation with the newly formed Federation of Malaysia. The formation of this new state was seen as a 'neo-colonial project designed by Great Britain'. These two military campaigns enhanced the army's prestige and helped ruin the country's economy.
4 Kartowiyono (1975) has analysed the implications of Sukarno's polygamy for the Indonesian women's movement in general and for Perwari, of which she was the chairperson in those years, in particular.
5 Langenberg (1986) has provided us with an interesting analysis of Indonesian government rhetoric.
6 Pancasila is the name of the official government philosophy. It is based on five principles which were originally formulated by Sukarno in 1945.
7 Gerwani members were said to have engaged themselves in 'obscene dancing', of 'mutilating the generals' genitals and of gouging out their eyes' on the field where the rebellious soldiers killed some generals. Subsequent reports indicated that Aidit (the chairman of the PKI) had had hundreds of Gerwani women trained to become prostitutes for the service of himself and other male party leaders. In cartoons which appeared for instance in the army newspaper, the PKI was pictured as a devil, with Gerwani written on its body.

References

ANDERSON, Ben (1987) 'How Did the Generals Die?' *Indonesia no. 43*, Ithaca: Cornell Southeast Asia Program.

CROUCH, Harold (1978) *The Army and Politics in Indonesia* Ithaca: Cornell University Press.

FEITH, Herbert (1962) *The Decline of Constitutional Democracy in Indonesia* Ithaca: Cornell University Press.

GUNAWAN, B. (1968) *Kudeta, staatsgreep in Djakarta, de achtergronden van de 30 september-beweging in Indonesie* Meppel: Boom.

KARTOWIYONO, Sujatin (1975) *Perkembangan pergerakan wanita Indonesia* Jakarta: Yayasan Idayu.

LANGENBERG, Michael Van (1986) 'Analysing Indonesia's New Order State: A Keywords Approach?' *RIMA, Review of Indonesian and Malaysian Affairs* Summer.

MAY, Brian (1978) *The Indonesian Tragedy* Singapore: Graham Brash.

MOENADI, Mrs (1971) *Family Welfare Education* Jakarta: Pendidikan Kesedjahteraan Keluarga (PKK).

MOLYNEUX, Maxine (1985) 'Mobilization Without Emancipation? Women's Interests, State and Revolution in Nicaragua' in SLATER (1985).

MORTIMER, Rex (1974) *Indonesian Communism Under Sukarno. Ideology and Politics 1959–65* Ithaca: Cornell University Press.

ROESTAM, Mrs Kardinah Soepardjo (1988) *Family Welfare Movement (PKK) in Indonesia and its Achievement* Jakarta: PKK.

RICKLEFS, M. C. (1981) *A History of Modern Indonesia, c 1300 to the present* London: Macmillan.

SARDJONO, Umi (1964) *Madju Terus untuk Pengintegrasian total Gerwani dengan Wanita Buruhtani dan Tanimiskin* Laporan kepada Sidang Pleno ke-III DPP Gerwani, Djkarta: DPP Gerwani.

SLATER, D (1985) *New Social Movements and the State in Latin America*, Amsterdam: CEDLA.

SUKARNO, Ir (1963) *Sarinah, Kewadjiban Waniua dalam Perdjoangan Republik Indonesia* Jakarta. Panitya penerbit buku-buku presiden Sukarno (Committee to publish the works of President Sukarno).

TÖRNQUIST, Olle (1984) *Dilemmas of Third World Communism: the destruction of the PKI in Indonesia* London: Zed Books.

WERTHEIM, W. F. (1978) *Van Vorstenrijk tot Neo-Kolonie* Amsterdam: Van Gennep.

—— (1985) *Wiens Samenzwering? Nieuw Licht op de Gebeurtenissen van 1965 in Indonesië: de Waarheid omtrent 1965*, Amsterdam: 'Indonesia Media'.

WIERINGA, Saskia (1981) 'En Overal laat zij Bloedsporen achter; Macht, sekse en Klasse in de Batikindustrie van Midden Java' *SocFem Teksten 5* Amsterdam: Sara.

—— (1985) *The Perfumed Nightmare, some Notes on the Indonesian Women's Movement* The Hague: ISS.

—— (1988a) 'Aborted Feminism in Indonesia, a History of Indonesian Socialist Feminism', in WIERINGA (1985).

—— (1988b) editor, *Women's Struggles and Strategies* London: Gower Press.

REPORT: 'MOTHERLANDS': Symposium on African, Caribbean, and Asian Women's Writing, 18–20 September 1991

Dorothea Smartt

'Motherlands' took place midweek, at the Institute of Commonwealth Studies (ICS), University of London. It was organized under the auspices of the ICS and financially assisted by Greater London Arts and the Arts Council. The two and a half days promised the opportunity to meet with, and discuss the ideas of some of the leading analysts of African, Caribbean and South Asian women writers together with some of the writers. The conference reception provided the launch of the book, *Motherlands*. The book was marketed as the work of African, Caribbean and South Asian writers, rather than as 'a cross-cultural dialogue between critics and writers' (Nasta, 1991: xviii).

The opening session attracted the largest numbers, with approximately fifty people crowded into the Menzies Room of the Institute. The chairs against the wall and around the oval conference table were filled predominantly, to my surprise and disappointment, with white women. Later I realized that the majority of the Black women present were authors, who were to feature in the four Writers' Readings of the symposium. Only five of the eighteen panellists were Black women; Ranjana Ash, Shirley Chew, Rhonda Cobham, Carolyn Cooper and Shahrukah Husain.

The opening Writers' Reading profiled Merle Collins, Leena Dhringa, Buchi Emecheta, and Marlene Nourbese Philip. Ms Collins read her poem 'Crick-crack . . .', which challenges the interpretations others offer of events in our lives that are then seen as fact – because *they* speak them. Ms Philip offered the riddles and anagrams of her new cross-genre narrative (Philip, 1991), on the 'silence' of indigenous peoples and David Livingstone's carrying of the white man's burden of interpretation.

Black women in attendance were reduced to around eight the following day. In the first panel, Elleke Boehmer discussed 'Motherland: Bond or Bind' a paper from the first part of her essay in *Motherlands* and Mary Kolaowle the 'Mother Motif in Nigerian Feminine Literature: the Myth and the Reality'. Caroline Rooney examined the 'Dangerous Knowledge' in the work of Bessie Head, and Jane Bryce presented 'Changes: Ama Ata Aidoo and Recent Writing by Ghanaian Women'.

For me, the most memorable presentation of the morning was Carolyn Cooper's 'Something Ancestral Recaptured: Spirit Possession as Trope in Selected Feminist Fictions of the African Diaspora', featured in *Motherlands*. She offered a sympathetic, insider treatment of a frequently misunderstood aspect of Caribbean life. A powerful vision of Afrocentric ideology reconstructed in the works of Una Marson, Erna Brodber, Paule Marshall, Sylvia Wynter, and Toni Morrison. The metaphors highlighted in Brodber's work, echoed those in Ms Collins's and Ms Philip's chosen readings, challenging and taking on the official version of history to reveal a perspective of our own.

The Writers' Reading for the second day featured poets Debjani Chatterjee and Elaine Fido (stepping out of academic mode), plus a last-minute contribution by Sindiwe Magona, with a welcome lively reading from her autobiography (1991). In the second panel Shirley Chew offered an afterword to her *Motherlands* contribution examining the work of Anita Desai and Nayantara Sahgal. Judie Newman's 'Post-Colonial Gothic' was an unconvincing reading of the text and subtext in the work of Ruth Prawer Jhabvala. The forthright Ranjana Ash offered her insights into 'The Theme of Motherland, My Land, in Three Indian Women Writers'. Writing on Nayantara Sahgal, Mahasveta Devi, and Amrita Pritam, she highlights an aspect of their work neglected by feminists; the concept of the female self as part of a national entity. The day closed with Jan Shinebourne, Lauretta Ngcobo, Leena Dhingra and Merle Collins relating their experiences of being published, chaired by publisher Margaret Busby. Ms Dhingra raised the issue of the lack of critical interest that plagues South Asian women writers.

On the final morning, Isabel Hoving put forward her interpretation of Jamaica Kincaid's work, reading *A Small Place* as a deconstruction of the discourse in *At the Bottom of the River* (Kincaid, 1984) and concluding that her earlier work is not the model of postmodern deconstruction it is held to be. Margaret Dunn looked at the complex concept of motherland in the works of such writers as Michelle Cliff and Jean Rhys. Lunchtime readers included Joan Riley and Pauline Melville. Joan Riley read extracts from her latest novel-in-progress in which she challenges notions of mothering in Caribbean life. She takes a class position, arguing for an unromanticized vision of the reality of the lives of Caribbean women, very different from the acceptable middle-class literary 'formula'.

The fourth and final panel of 'Motherlands' gave us a considered meditation by Rhonda Cobham in which she explored migration as metaphor for the disorientation of shifting gender and national boundaries, in works by Tsitsi Dangaremba and Bessie Head. Isabel Carrera Suarez offered an interpretation of Joan Riley's fiction as female-centred studies of loss; 'Absent Mother(Lands) and No Romance'. Elaine Fido's departure from her manuscript (an attempt to develop a theory of Caribbean women's writing) was a rare moment, in which she challenged her peers saying 'never to falsify, never to forget' you are white women, writing about Black women. For some dealing with symbols, not experience, is a passport to exclude and even invalidate the critical responses of Black women to their literature.

The final Writers' Reading was chaired by the symposium organizer Susheila Nasta. Its make-up suggested generations of writers, with words from Beryl Gilroy, Suniti Namjoshi and Lauretta Ngcobo. Beryl Gilroy reminded us that she was first published in the 1950s. Ms Namjoshi played with the term 'Motherland' and also raised, if only momentarily, the visibility of lesbian writing and writers at this symposium.

The two days were (antagonistically) inspiring, for writer and critic alike. Stimulating, exciting, depressing, threatening and always challenging (as the text disappeared one minute, and the writer the next). Was the title 'Motherlands' used in obvious irony? It is a paradoxical title for a symposium (and a book) where most of the contributors are of the imperial 'Motherlands', and are still speaking for the 'natives', translating them for the Empire (of academia).

Susheila Nasta said she shared my disappointment at the lack of Black women present. She had mailed out to community centres and Black bookshops. As for the make-up of the book's contributors, she had sent out forty-odd letters to women from a variety of backgrounds and *Motherlands* represents the respondents.

The Institute is not the most accessible of buildings. I have visited there before, and even recommended other Black women to go there. But always with words of caution as the women at the reception desk seem determined to maintain its élite exclusivity, even when a publicly funded event is held there. Perhaps the organizers were unaware that, before being invited to give a name and address for a registration form, callers were queried as to how they heard about the symposium, and which institution they were affiliated with. Questions that left me asking who is this symposium for? Regardless of how many community centres and Black bookshops receive notices, that interaction may (sadly) tell all you need to know about who they expect to be there.

Overall the symposium perpetuated the 'whiteness' and Eurocentrism of literary criticism. The focus of some papers seemed to be to 'fit' Black women's writing into a 'feminist' understanding of women's writing and traditional female forms. An imperialist 'feminist' understanding, with the prime aim to deliver work into the experience and understanding of the European reader and writer and as such to 'universalize' Black women's writing. Black women reading and replying to Black writers, from a shared understanding of diasporic experience and culture, from inside that shared 'cultural confidence', with its own class, caste, gender and colour codes, was sadly a minority perspective. British Black women writing about Black women's literature were made 'unknown', invisible to the participants.

The perceptions of white women *about* the worlds created by Black women were validated, in the sense that they would be public, recorded and presented in a format most likely to reach a wider audience, a more decisive audience for the publisher's sales than any perceptions by Black women themselves. As such, they design the spaces, and shape the discussions we will most likely be asked to address or refer to (if only in the negative).

Their presumption of the right to speak on and proclaim creates a contemporary parallel to Philip's 'Livingstone I presume'.

PS For Black women reading this

To paraphrase Barbara Smith, I know you're out there, probably isolated, reading this. Do we have time to deliberate on and on? Turning our sistah's words inside out. Unloading, unfolding the messages of our griot sistahs. I call-out for those of you enjoying reading their writing, and like me, discussing and writing about the literature. I ask myself why aren't you here? (knowing full well some of the reasons why); can we connect? To create the opportunities to muse over ourselves, the meanings of our writers, speaking to us, for us, voicing our concerns, our happenings, our hopes and fears. We do have something worthwhile to say and they have had the monopoly too long. Their days are numbered. Box 17, 124 Vassall Road, London SW9 6JB.

References

KINCAID, Jamaica (1984) *At the Bottom of the River* London: Picador.
—— (1988) *A Small Place* London: Virago.
MAGONA, Sindiwe (1991) *To My Children's Children* London: Women's Press.
NASTA, Susheila (1991) editor, *Motherlands: Black Women's Writing from Africa, the Caribbean and South Asia* London: Women's Press.
PHILIP, Nourbese Marlene (1991) *Looking for Livingstone: An Odyssey of Silence* Ontario: Mercury Press.

REPORT: THE EUROPEAN FORUM OF SOCIALIST FEMINISTS Norwich, 1991

Irene Bruegel

'What we sought, while you in the West were pursuing collective demands, was the right to decent make-up, the right to express ourselves as individuals: after all we *had* the collective provisions and formal rights you were after. We suffered a lack of individual rights. The things you take for granted.' In this mirror image Zarana Papic from Yugoslavia captured something of the mutual understanding and misunderstanding between feminists from Eastern and Western Europe who met in Norwich in June 1991 for the sixth European Forum of Socialist Feminists. Over a hundred women came from twenty countries in all, with representation extending from Iceland to Greece and beyond.

Difficulties of establishing a common understanding between socialist feminists from different parts of Europe were not new to the Feminist Forum. While each of the meetings of the Forum has established a warm, positive and very precious feeling of international sisterhood, building an understanding of each other's perspectives has proved a slow and difficult process, especially as the Forum progressively sought to reach beyond the north-west corner of Europe and to involve women from outside academia.

Back in 1986 when women from Britain had first raised the need to put issues of race and nationality on the agenda, they were greeted with blank looks, from Nordic and Southern European sisters. Equally the first East European women to attend the Forum, in Gothenburg in 1989, just after the Berlin Wall came down, were clearly uncomfortable with any discussion of sexuality. However, by 1991 it proved possible to organize a conference specifically around the theme of women and citizenship, in which the politics of lesbian sexuality had an accepted place. Issues of racism and nationality were to be a central part of the agenda in Norwich. Despite the very unequal numbers, the Norwich Forum was in some ways as much a meeting ground of black and white women as of Eastern and Western women, with the inherent tensions of such a juxtaposition, but also with a remarkable degree of mutual recognition.

For the white East European women at the Forum the issue of racial discrimination was first and foremost that of their own experiences, both as foreigners in other Eastern Bloc countries and in encounters with the West. They recognized that groups of women in their own countries – gypsies, Muslims and Jews in particular – encountered discrimination, but this was remote from their immediate concerns as feminists. Their own sensitivity to being seen as poor relations in the West came through much more strongly. Much as they valued the chance to meet other feminists, they saw strands of ethnocentrism lurking in Western feminism and began to question the assumption that we were to be the model for their feminism. Picking up, indeed, on our learning to acknowledge difference, the feminists from Eastern Europe sought time to talk amongst themselves at the Forum and determined to hold a conference for feminists from the Eastern Bloc countries alone before the next full Forum gathering. They wanted practical help from us – financial support for the first Feminist journal in Czechoslovakia and solidarity action in support of their campaigns – not any prescription about what path to pursue. Much of this discussion echoed that between Western and Third World feminists over the last decade, or more.

The issue of identity became paramount at Norwich. We could accept that feminism was not in principle incompatible with a demand from women in the East for more time with their children, or for better-quality make-up; that what is important is women's self-activity towards an 'emancipation' defined by women themselves, each in their specific circumstances. But how elastic a concept could it be? Could you be a feminist and argue as one Czech woman sought to do 'that men in Eastern Europe had suffered a loss of self-esteem and identity under Communist rule', and that there was 'now a need for them to assert themselves as men'? We found ourselves much more able to respond to Beata Grudzinska from Poland calling for support in their defence of abortion rights and the view that feminism had to be unequivocally and actively opposed to fundamentalism in whatever religious guise.

The Forum had been designed to explore the relationship between feminism and nationalism, an issue which was made all the more immediate as the troop movements prevented the Slovenian/Yugoslav representative attending at the last minute. But many of the women at the Forum seemed perplexed by the primacy an Irish woman gave to the struggle for national liberation. The debate on nationalism and national liberation movements familiar to Third World feminism had barely permeated East/West discussion. Nationalism was to be resisted; what was important was to find communalities of identity as women from many different countries.

Our identity as socialists had for long been a sensitive issue. From the very beginning in 1985 it was clear that within and between countries, feminists interpreted the Forum's socialist identity very differently. Some of the initial cross-national links had been established by women who at one time or other had been associated with the Trotskyist Fourth International; other women came from small beleaguered Communist parties in the West, though most came as individuals with no party affiliations. For them socialist feminism was defined more in counterposition to radical or bourgeois feminism than as any tight party line. Despite this *mélange* of positions in relation to mainstream 'socialisms', the Forum was an arena where feminists have been able to learn from one another, to move, slowly perhaps, towards a common agenda, but at Norwich the hitherto fudged question of whether we should continue to identify ourselves as socialist feminists could no longer be avoided.

It wasn't a new issue; feminists from Spain and Greece had argued long before 1989 that the name should be changed because it did not reflect their reality. It identified them wrongly with the ruling Social Democratic parties; others of us saw any change of name as a concession to New-Times-speak, a repackaging for greater consumer appeal, covering over an inevitable revision of principles.

Some of the Eastern European women argued that to retain the 'socialist' title would make it impossible to build links with feminists in the East. There was a sense of affront in not acknowledging the horrors of 'actually existing socialism', of how women's aspirations and liberation had been mangled in the name of 'socialism'. On the other hand many women from Eastern Europe recognized that what *we* meant by socialism had no affinity at all with what had actually existed; that there was value in fighting to reclaim 'socialism' for ourselves. The debate was heated and not resolved, remitted to the 1992 Forum to be held in Brussels. For all that, for many of us it was the most fruitful discussion we have had for years. We had gone beyond the euphoria of meeting real live feminists from 'over there', towards a deepening understanding of the problems we both faced and an acute awareness of the difficulties of supporting one another positively in increasingly hostile conditions.

For further information about FORUM contact: Cynthia Cockburn, 83 Bartholomew Road, London NW5.

REVIEWS

Feminism and Youth Culture: From Jackie to Just Seventeen

Angela McRobbie

Macmillan: London 1991, £9.99 Pbk
ISBN 0 333 45264 X, £35.00 Hbk
ISBN 0 333 45263 1

Schoolgirl Fictions

Valerie Walkerdine.

Verso: London 1991, £10.95 Pbk
ISBN 0 86091 517 4, £32.95 Hbk
ISBN 0 86091 299 X

Unfortunately, the first thought that came to mind when looking at these two collections of feminist essays was – I seem to have read most of this stuff before . . .

While these 'new' scholarly collections share an emphasis on the often neglected subject of working-class female adolescence, both books, because they contain such a lot of reprinted material, at first sight do appear to be disappointingly 'retrospective'. For instance, both McRobbie and Walkerdine included material in these 1991 volumes which previously made a debut in the 1984 Macmillan collection *Gender and Generation*.[1] However, the largely reprinted nature of these 'new' collections does not invalidate them or mean they are not useful.

'Very little has been said about the role of girls in youth cultural groupings' commented Angela McRobbie and Jenny Garber in 1978.[2] Thirteen years later Angela McRobbie has significantly contributed to changing this situation. This new book gathers together eight essays about the lived experience of girls in youth culture and popular culture. By presenting previously published work in this way McRobbie offers readers of *Feminism and Youth Culture* cultural analysis and careful ethnography in the context of the development of her own ideas.

Despite the fact that some of the empirical examples in this collection look a little dated, the writing *is* accessible and raises many theoretical questions about the behaviour of working-class girls that still require attention today. This is largely because McRobbie's writing, past and present, rarely offers a simple interpretation of why female experience had been marginalized by early subcultural theorists.

Essays like 'Settling Accounts with Subculture', included here but first published in 1980 were of seminal influence.[3] This particular essay was written when McRobbie was at the Centre for Contemporary Cultural Studies at Birmingham University. Her writing from that period, as she indicates in the Introduction, was inspired by the moment when interdisciplinary perspectives were brought to bear on the study of culture, defined by Raymond Williams not as something saved for Sunday best, but as 'a whole way of life'. Here, McRobbie's work was significant because her emphasis on ordinary femininity made a serious contribution to the debate which located gender as something 'cultural' rather than 'natural'.

Indeed, McRobbie broke new ground when she suggested girls' position in youth subcultures like Teds and Mods had either been ignored or inappropriately described as one of passivity by male researchers.[4] She went on to identify how in classic subcultural studies the street life of working-class boys had been overprivileged at the expense of discussion of family life, domestic labour and the structural position of gender ideologies.

Yet the essays in *Feminism and Youth Culture* do not go on, as some readers may anticipate, to look at how these issues affected analysis of female participation in more recent youth cultural groupings. For instance, this book doesn't consider the role of young women in more recent subcultures, from the New Romantics to Acid House.[5] Instead, McRobbie moves on to write about teenagers and consumerism, an intellectual strategy which is extremely relevant since subculture doesn't mean what it did.

In the nineties – when authentic subcultural activity seems to change so quickly – youth style appears to have more in common with lifestyle marketing employed by advertising and the fashion industry, than with a 'counter-cultural' space outside of consumerism. (Nowadays many young people have been through more than one subcultural experience before they are out of their teens.) Although McRobbie doesn't come right out and state in this collection exactly why she moved away from straightforward discussion of subcultures to focus on other issues raised by youth consumerism, there are hints in the

early essays that demonstrate the astute perception underlying her shift of emphasis.

In 1978 McRobbie insisted that critics should not really get caught up in counting the presence or absence of girls in street gangs but instead should try and understand the way young women form their own subcultures, and how these are understood and accommodated by girls' magazines.[6] This focus appears to have provided the impetus for much of McRobbie's subsequent work which is preoccupied with unravelling the contradictory aspect of the authentic and the manufactured nature of teenage culture as well as decoding the meaning of style.

By studying girls' magazines – from *Jackie* to *Just Seventeen* – and the way teenage girls make sense of them, McRobbie takes seriously the function of fantasy. In 'Teenage Mothers: A New Social State', a new essay written for this collection, she also considers economic questions when she assesses well-documented ground about the consequence of the allure of motherhood for working-class girls in the context of antischool subcultures. Yet it is McRobbie's analysis of the commodification of teenage daydreams by comics that continues to be controversial (if Martin Barker's recent criticisms in *Comics, Power and Ideology* (1989) are anything to go by).[7] This approach to the discussion of fantasy, which may appear eclectic to those not familiar with cultural-studies methodology, is important not least because McRobbie begins to raise questions taken up by the theorists of the so-called postmodern age.[8]

Similar concerns about young women and their relationship to school and fantasy are also raised by Valerie Walkerdine in *Schoolgirl Fictions*, which includes twenty essays written between 1981 and 1989. Walkerdine's methodology differs from McRobbie's, however, because as well as including autobiographical fragments and poetry Walkerdine privileges a psychoanalytic reading of popular culture forms (which she measures against empirical data and her own experience) to investigate gender as fiction.

Schoolgirl Fictions is separated into three sections. The first contains essays written between 1981 and 1985 and looks at unwitting bias embedded in pedagogic strategies (Walkerdine, 1989). This section commences with 'Sex, Power and Pedagogy', an essay which sets out to challenge the idea that pupils are powerless in the classroom. Walkerdine's investigation of the discourse of young boys considers how male pupils are easily able to 'resist the authority of female teachers (speech like 'Miss Baxter show your knickers off')' by utilizing patriarchal narratives about sexual objectification. It contrasts how female pupils are virtually silenced by the subjectivities constructed for them by pedagogic definitions and expectations.

These ideas are further developed in 'Science and the Female Mind', another essay in which Walkerdine identifies some of the gender fictions that abound in the classroom. She says these gender fictions place different expectations on boys and girls in relation to subjects like mathematics: 'in spite of obvious success girls' performance is constantly demonstrated to be different . . . the idea that difference is in some way a deficiency, surfaces time after time.' Other essays on educational themes, which may be familiar to *Feminist Review* readers, go on to develop Walkerdine's analysis of power/knowledge in education which she says 'cannot be understood historically outside considerations about gender'.

Sections two and three of *Schoolgirl Fictions*, written between 1984 and 1989 about popular culture and working-class childhood did not follow on easily from the earlier educational emphasis. Despite the fact the author had written new prefaces to bind material together the

sequence was, at times, difficult to follow other than chronologically. On the whole, the inclusion of fragments of autobiography made the otherwise academic tone of the book, which addresses poststructuralist issues about subjectivity, much more readable. Sometimes I felt Walkerdine's inclusion of personal experience really fleshed out dry psychoanalytic observations and managed to inject vibrant colour to the monochromic specificity of empirical evidence. Other articles, about working-class lives, which were also autobiographical in focus, were perhaps too earnest about the past. They seemed to concentrate upon uncovering forgotten emotions rather than taking the opportunity to include specific historical detail.

To summarize the rest of the book: section two examined narratives about gender represented in popular culture. Essays like 'One Day My Prince Will Come',[9] examined fictions about femininity available in teenage comics and still managed to offer a persuasive discussion about the influence romantic fantasies have upon teenage years, despite the fact that I had read a lot of this material before. (This point is also addressed by McRobbie.) Similarly 'Behind the Painted Smile' – an essay which is incidentally also reprinted in the Virago collection on photography (Spence and Hollands, 1991) – raised many questions about photographic fictions which obscure complicated emotions beneath the surfaces of smiling portraits. This was one of my favourite pieces as I felt it managed to get the balance right when discussing the relationship of the personal to the political.

'I felt in the old place, as in the new, that if I opened my mouth it would be to say the wrong things', Walkerdine comments in section three about feeling out of step with the cultural formations she encounters (a feeling this reviewer recognizes only too well). This final section contains Walkerdine's 'look back in anger' at working-class culture in the form of autobiographical pieces about the author's painful journey between the two worlds of then and now. While I identified with many of the complicated emotions involved in Walkerdine no longer feeling completely at home in either the clothes of the working-class schoolgirl or the middle-class academic,[10] I think the generational gap showed in these retrospective articles. Walkerdine's emphasis on discourse theory and 'fictions of gender' to explain her experiences in the academy were persuasive but unable directly to address the financial hardships faced by contemporary working-class students or part-time lecturers.

Today's Women's Studies students – including lesbian, working-class and black women – hopefully have more space to speak about the alienation that comes from engaging with white/male/middle-class (or even feminist) epistemologies than Walkerdine may have had. For them, and lecturers without tenure, however, economic issues affecting education are far more biting than they were in the sixties and seventies. In the nineties, for instance, grant or part-time lecturing income doesn't adequately cover research time required and there are literally not enough books in poly libraries adequately to accommodate students who cannot afford to buy some of their own.

So despite my genuine respect for the feminist scholars and the positive elements of their books reviewed here, I find it necessary to separate text from context in order to discuss the material fully. Indeed, the appearance of two reprinted feminist collections at the same time did raise questions for me about the politics underlying the publishing of reissued material.

It may be true that Women's Studies lists are now being offered by academic publishers more than ever before and there is demand for material. But at a time when feminist research grants are being cut and autonomous feminist publishing is in decline,[11] it is perhaps worrying that the live feminist scholarly reprint looks set to oust or supplement the trend for reprinting the novels of dead women. (A phenomenon pioneered by Virago[12] and copied by British publishers including left houses.)

In the 1990s I suspect we will be reading or reviewing many feminist essays the second time around *and at the right cover price this is no bad thing*. But cover prices are high, and given that most academic publishers don't pay authors the sort of advances that would be needed to finance new research, I would call for feminists who do allow their work to be reprinted to think about where else it is available. For example, I have some of the articles in these two 'new' books in two other places, and feel disappointed, or dare I say it, short-changed by this.

Indeed, it is about time publishers were pressurized to reduce prices of books made up almost entirely of reissued material. I may be a cynic but I am not convinced that this recycling and reprinting provides a true indication of renewed interest in feminism. It seems likely that the live feminist scholarly reprint developed as a phenomenon not only because feminist thinkers are at last becoming recognized, but because it constitutes low-investment publishing. Obviously authors have their own reasons for authorizing the reissue of their work[13] and so it would be inappropriate to say that reprints constitute 'exploitation' or simply another publishing 'scam'. Yet in the rush to reprint the past, both publishers and authors should take care to ensure that feminism doesn't look like it has run out of new ideas or fresh ways to express them.

Lorraine Gamman

Notes

1 This collection is out of print.
2 Quote from McRobbie (1979) which originally appeared in Hall (1978).
3 This article originally appeared in *Screen Education* (1980) No. 39.
4 Cohen (1972); Willis (1977); Hebdidge (1979)
5 For those interested there is discussion about this in contemporary subculture: McRobbie (1989). There is also some excellent writing on women and punk in Evans and Thornton (1990). Brake (1985) offers a good summary of early writing on girls and subculture.
6 'Girls and Subcultures' essay in McRobbie (1991: 11).
7 Barker (1989). These criticisms seem to be adapted from an earlier article: Martin Barker, (1986) 'Methods For Cultural Studies Students' in Punter D.
8 Angela McRobbie has contributed journalism to debates about postmodernism including an article in Lisa Appignanesi., editor, (1986) *Postmodernism*, ICA Document 4 published in association with Free Association Books.
9 First published in McRobbie and Nava (1984).
10 Similar impulses, that is achieving some social mobility but still finding certain doors closed, originally made sixties new wave playwrights – like Osborne. – angry in the first place. In Walkerdine's book, patriarchal, as well as class relations, incite her anger in terms of the way they create an impasse in some academic structures and epistemologies.
11 See publishing overview presented by Helen Birch.
12 I am personally not against the publishing of artistically or historically significant reprints. But I think the points made by Rebecca O'Rourke in 'Summer Reading' (*Feminist Review*, No. 2) that 'commercial publishers are cashing in on feminism', raised again by Ros Coward on p. 235 of Showalter (1986) are still relevant.
13 Williamson (1991) outlines the 'publish or perish' philosophy. Her article argues British higher education is following the American precedent whereby publishing is what is valued rather than teaching practice.

References

BARKER, Martin (1989) *Comics, Power and Ideology* Manchester: Manchester University Press.

BIRCH, Helen (1991) 'Bold Types in a Buyers Market', *New Statesman* 31 May.

BRAKE, Michael (1985) *Comparative Youth Culture* London: Routledge & Kegan Paul.

COHEN, Stanley (1972) *Folk Devils and Moral Panics: The Creation of the Mods and Rockers* London: MacGibbon & Kee.

EVANS, Caroline and THORNTON, Minna (1990) *Women and Fashion: A New Look* London: Quartet.

HALL, Stuart (1978) editor, *Resistance Through Ritual* London: Unwin Hyman. Reprinted 1989.

HEBDIGE, Dick (1979) *Subculture: The Meaning of Style* London: Methuen.

MCROBBIE, Angela (1979) 'Girls and Subcultures' in HALL (1978).

—— (1989) editor, *Zoot Suits and Second Hand Dresses* Basingstoke: Macmillan.

—— (1991) *Feminism and Youth Culture* Basingstoke: Macmillan.

MCROBBIE, Angela and NAVA, Mica (1984) editors, *Gender and Generation* Basingstoke: Macmillan.

PUNTER, D (1986) editor, *Contemporary Cultural Studies* London: Longman.

SHOWALTER, E. (1986) editor, *The New Feminist Criticism* London: Virago.

SPENCE, Jo and Patricia HOLLANDS, (1991) editors *Family Snaps: The Meaning of Domestic Photography* London: Virago.

WALKERDINE, Valerie (1989) *Counting Girls Out* London: Virago.

—— (1991) *Schoolgirl Fictions* London: Macmillan.

WILLIAMSON, Judith (1991) 'Never Mind the Quality Think for Yourself' *The Guardian* 25 April.

WILLIS, Paul (1977) *Learning to Labour* Farnborough: Saxon House.

From Abortion to Reproductive Freedom: Transforming A Movement
Edited by Marlene Gerber Fried
South End Press: Boston 1990 £8.95
ISBN 0 89608 387 X Pbk

The Supreme Court ruling on Roe v. Wade in 1973 was as significant to American women as the passing of the 1967 Abortion Act was for women in Britain. It legalized abortion. Since 1973 some 25 million women have had legal abortions in the USA. The Roe ruling was based on the right to privacy – any state interference into the doctor–patient relationship and into a woman's procreation decisions was considered violations of that right.

From Abortion to Reproductive Freedom: Transforming a Movement is an anthology, unprecedented in its cultural diversity, which offers an historical and critical account of the abortion rights movement from the late 1960s to the present day. This book is not just about fighting for abortion rights, though it is no coincidence that it was conceived during the period when the Webster v. Reproductive Health Services decision was pending. The subsequent Supreme Court ruling on this case, taken in July 1989, effectively eroded Constitutional protections for abortion. The Court upheld a Missouri law restricting abortion, saying that 'the life of each human being begins at conception' and agreed that individual states had the right to prohibit both 'public facilities' and 'public employees' from being used to perform or assist abortions not required to save the life of the pregnant woman. The Webster decision has paved the way for continued attacks on abortion rights at state level and the real possibility of overturning Roe altogether.

In the USA during the two decades which have followed Roe, there's been a slow chipping away of the gains made by the pro-choice movement. The 1977 Hyde Amendment prohibited federal Medicaid funding of abortion which was to have a serious affect on access to termination, particularly for low-income women. Despite being a serious blow to abortion rights, critics have observed that the Hyde Amendment did not whip up the type of street demonstrations and political action reminiscent of the sixties. The full force of the pro-choice movement only re-emerged to regain its pre-Roe activism because of real threats to recriminalize abortion in the 1980s. On Sunday 9 April 1989 the

pro-choice movement showed its real strength by mounting a 600,000-person-strong march and rally in Washington DC in support of Roe v. Wade and the Equal Rights Amendment. The March for Women's Equality and Women's Lives was organized by the National Organization for Women to coincide with the latest attack on Roe.

Attacks on abortion rights in the USA have been an opportunity for many reproductive-rights activists to reassess a movement in the light of broader issues affecting women. It's no surprise this right-wing backlash has taken place. In the USA the judiciary have the power to make and break laws, whereas in Britain, Parliament has to vote on these issues. The majority of all federal judges and almost half the Supreme Court Justices have been appointed by the Reagan/Bush administrations. But will the fightback and demands be narrow or broad?

Beyond abortion rights, this anthology is about differences, alliances and coalition-building. It's about a vision of the future which allows for activism around reproductive-rights issues that affect all women and is essential reading for all feminists and others interested in women's struggle for reproductive freedom.

The book is organized into four sections: 'The Politics of the Abortion Rights Movement'; 'Speaking Out for Women: Choosing Ourselves'; 'Defending Abortion Rights: Confronting Threats to Access'; and 'Expanding the Agenda: Building an Inclusive Movement'. The problem about reviewing this anthology is that there are so many diverse and compelling contributions, that it's difficult to give an overall flavour. This is particularly true because, as the title suggests, the book transcends abortion rights. The radical solution is nothing less than reproductive freedom for all women. This is a very tall order and so the anthology addresses a wide number of

issues, including: teenage pregnancy, defending abortion clinics
from attack, infant mortality,
struggles of Puerto Rican women,
lesbian and gay issues, disability
rights, AIDS and women's health in
the so-called Third World.

The book's contributors include
a wide variety of activists, health
workers, lawyers, academics and
journalists. Some are well-known
writers, like Angela Davis who addresses the issue of racism in the
abortion-rights and birth-control
movements by focusing on eugenics,
population control, and sterilization
abuse. Others are not so well known
outside the USA, like Byllye Avery,
Director and founder of the National
Black Women's Health Project in
Atlanta who relates her moving experiences of helping women to obtain
abortions before and after Roe.

In order to address the diversity
of reproductive-rights issues the
book affirms the necessity to broaden
the base of a movement and to widen
the agenda in which 'choice' and
'rights' have real meaning for all
women, not just those who have
economic control over their lives. In
the introduction the anthology editor
and long-time reproductive-rights
activist, Marlene Gerber Fried, explains the background to the book:
'Transforming the abortion rights
movement from a relatively narrow
one focused on defending the legal
right to abortion to a movement for
reproductive freedom, from a movement whose membership and leadership is predominantly white to an
inclusive movement with a broad
and diverse grassroots base, these
are key political tasks facing reproductive rights activists. And these
are the issues that motivated this
book.'

There are some striking statistics in the book which reveal how
unhealthy it is to be a poor woman in
the richest nation on earth. The
chapter entitled 'The Reproductive
Health of Black Women and Other
Women of Colour' (p. 157) dispels

many myths about black women's
health including the misconception
that black women don't have abortions.

● In 1969, for example, 75 per cent
of the women who died from illegal
abortions were women of colour.
● Women of colour constitute over
30 per cent of Title X patients, the
ones who will be denied information about the abortion option
under the federal regulation
upheld by the Supreme Court in
Rust v. Sullivan (1991). 32 per
cent of the Title X patients are
adolescents.
● Since the Michigan State Legislature outlawed state Medicaid
funding for abortion last year, at
least ten low-income women have
been admitted to one Detroit hospital alone for treatment of injuries resulting from attempts to
self-abort. (National Organization
of Women)

If anyone is in doubt about the
inequalities of the land of the free, a
trip through this chapter will make
it numerically clear equality and
choice are options for those who can
afford them.

Given these glaring inequalities, why aren't low-income women
and women of colour in the leadership of the reproductive-rights and
pro-choice movements? One reason
is echoed by many contributors. For
too long, with the exception of a
radical, more politically aware
element, white women activists in
the abortion movement have under-
valued the participation of women of
colour in the reproductive-rights
movement. One of the contributors
to the book, Brenda Joyner of the
Tallahassee Feminist Women's
Health Center, describes herself as
identifying as a feminist for twenty
years but, she explains, not the kind
of feminist being promoted in mainstream organizations. She explains
the position of many black activists:
'Perhaps the question is not really
where are women of color in the

abortion rights and reproductive rights movement. Rather, where is the primarily white middle-class movement in our struggles for freedom? Where was a white middle-class movement when the Hyde Amendment took away Medicaid funding of abortions for poor women?' (p. 210) For Brenda and others, there can be no involvement in political organizations which do not address 'racism, classism and élitism'. She points out the Hyde Amendment only attacked poor women whereas Webster attacks all women's right to abortion. If there were 600,000 people on the streets over Hyde, perhaps Webster would not have happened.

But the book offers more than just criticism, it poses a revolutionary challenge to the reproductive-rights movement in the USA to become more radical in its demands. It questions the defensive 'right to privacy' argument which has dominated the political agenda of the leading pro-choice organizations in the USA, explaining that this has ignored black women's struggle. Abortion is just one in a long line of struggles for black women. Many contributors to the book are critical of a pro-choice movement which uses ambiguous language of 'choice' and 'personal freedom'. For these terms to take on any real purpose societal changes are needed. Fighting for reproductive rights for all women must include making the personal political again. It does not mean hiding behind the liberal veil of individuality.

The final section of the book illustrates how the struggle for reproductive freedom takes different forms in different communities. The issues raised cover the endless misery women face because of inequality and injustice.

For those of us engaged in struggles around reproductive rights in Britain, we would do well to read this book and take many notes. Many of us did see the limitations of single-issue campaigns like the National Abortion Campaign. It is clear abortion has never been the only issue. The need to change the political agenda from abortion rights to a reproductive-rights movement led to a split within NAC and the setting up of a broader based Reproductive Rights Campaign. Several years on we face the same fragmentation as our sisters in the USA. We may not face the same kind of violent anti-abortion movement, or the kind of intervention possible by the Supreme Court. Nevertheless, we have faced serious threats to abortion in the form of various Private Members' Bills, and the NHS still only performs less than 50 per cent of the total in England and Wales each year. The Human Fertilization and Embryology Bill reduced the time limit for abortion to 24 weeks and restricts access to infertility treatment or donor insemination through its 'welfare of the child' clause, which specifically refers to the 'need of the child for a father'. There are many battles for us to fight but how do we win the war for reproductive freedom? It's not easy to transform a movement, as the contributors to this book illustrate so eloquently. This anthology is a rich source of those and for those who are trying hard to make it happen.

Glynis Donovan

The Change: Women, Ageing and the Menopause

Germaine Greer

Hamish Hamilton: London 1991, £16.99, ISBN 0 241 12840 4 Hbk

Germaine Greer's newest book on menopause is as difficult to chart, as uneven, unpredictable and fascinating as the subject itself. She refers to the menopause as a taboo subject, a misunderstood 'time of life' needing exploration, demystification and re-definition. Quite rightly she lays bare the medical profession's lack of any coherent understanding or knowledge of the physiology or psychology of 'the change'. She explains, in great detail, what is known of the physiological developments which happen during the varied number of years each individual woman goes through it. She explores the relationship between the use of hormone replacement therapy (HRT) and fear of ageing (changing). Many feminists, old and new, are now approaching or have gone through 'the change'. We're experiencing what Greer is exploring; it addresses us, or those who can imagine its onset. That goes a long way in explaining why reactions to the book are so varied and strong. What younger women make of it is not important to Greer.

However, and somewhat contradictorily (but when isn't she contradictory?), Greer has stated that she didn't write this book for a target audience or for anyone in particular. She is not, she says, a feminist spokeswoman. It is her strength and weakness that she almost always writes out of her own experience, going on to construct huge generalizations and peppering the work with bits and bobs from anthropology, literature, medicine and psychology. Because she is an interesting, provocative writer she gets away with a heady mix of murder, mayhem and profundity, all delivered in the full blaze of public fascination.

Greer believes that the notion of 'no change' at menopause serves the continuation of women's subjugation to men. She sees the climacteric as being composed of three periods, 'two that exist and one that does not; the first is the peri-menopause, the time leading up to and the last bleed, the second is the menopause proper, the bleed that does not come, and the third is the post menopause. The critical time corresponds with the fifth climacter of a woman's life, the fifth of her seven ages.'

Does she or doesn't she believe in biological destiny for women? She posits motherhood as the most naturally achieved, naturally powerful position for women to hold in society, so it seems the answer is yes. In the chapter entitled 'The Lucky Ones' Greer describes 'traditional' societies in which mothers and grandmothers have defined and powerful roles to play, and in relation to these romanticized anthropological tidbits says, 'We can only wonder how much less women might suffer at menopause if they were to acquire power, prestige and responsibility instead of losing all three.' Yes, but why should this most 'naturally' happen via motherhood and a powerful role in the family sphere?

Speaking of possibilities for older women, Greer states that, 'We might develop better strategies for the management of the difficult transition if we think of what we are doing not as denial of the change or postponement of the change, but as acceleration of the change, the change back into the self you were before you became a tool of your sexual and reproductive destiny.'

Basically *The Change* represents a romanticized version of traditional societies in which women had an honoured and powerful place via motherhood and where the menopause did not signal loss of the double-edged methods women in 'modern' societies have developed to cope with their biological and sexual destinies. These modern women, Greer says, have only the sexual attractiveness of youth, or relationships with their husband or employer, and because the state has taken over the socialization of children, they have no meaningful mothering role except drudgery. However, Greer states, it's no wonder, that Western, 'modern' women resist the menopause, because the nature of the change is almost always perceived as loss, deficiency, invisibility, even if the reality is a sham.

In contrast, Greer suggests a radical shake-up in our perception of old age and the change. 'The change hurts. Like a person newly released from leg-irons, the freed woman staggers at first. Though her excessive visibility was anguish, her present invisibility is disorienting'. Greer scalpels Simone de Beauvoir's attitude to old age in one of the book's most interesting analyses of famous older women: 'Every day she told herself, "I am not what I was" and wasted precious time in bitter regret.'

What Greer gives us is a picture of women bowed down by their husbands' sexual demands, receiving attention only because of their youthful sexual attractiveness, with possibility for meaningful relationships restricted to the husband or the employer, under the sway of an ill-defined biological destiny. And then, up pops the change, another biological imperative, which in itself 'should' signal possibilities of freedom from the 'leg-irons'. The loss of sexual attractiveness to men 'should' mean freedom from sexual demands, it 'should' signal the possibility of sombre independence, of meeting one's own needs, not the powerless servicing of others' needs. 'In modern nuclear families there is only one relationship of intimacy and importance and that is the relationship between spouses. If that does not work the family must be jettisoned. The modern woman has only two possible sources of satisfaction, her

relationship with her husband and her relationship with her employer.' But older modern women are not, because of sexism and ageism, able to see the positive side of the menopause. 'She has a choice, to become the kind of stentorian bully who can be heard apostrophizing saleswomen from the other side of the store, or to fade out of sight and hearing.'

It would be silly to refute totally the dreary, depressing, put-upon picture Greer paints of women's lives in our society; however, it is profoundly depressing that Greer has chosen to ignore the impact of feminism on women, and to an extent, men, in our 'modern' societies. Friendship between women at any stage of their lives is almost absent in the Greer scenario. Friendships forged through feminism, friendships developed in neighbourhoods, through motherhood, through work, or in lesbian cultures, have no place of pride in the female guide to surviving well in a sexist and ageist society.

And what about lesbianism? No, not every book, on any subject, has to include lesbians. (Although an awareness and acknowledgement of assumed heterosexuality would be welcome.) However, in a book which includes a chapter on hardy perennials (this one got all the publicity because of its cutting remarks about well-known celebrities, although, since women like Joan Collins and Jane Fonda have put themselves in the limelight as role models for older women, taking them down a peg or two seems fair enough to me), as well as ones on the aged wife, the lucky ones, etc., the absence of lesbians is glaring. Lesbians go through the change, lesbians are not in sexual relationships with men. Wouldn't it have been interesting to ask whether or not the changes most of them have made before their menopause, but within a sexist and ageist society, have had any impact on how they see themselves – in the world and sexually?

But Greer embraces the end of

sexual relationships and because this is based entirely within a heterosexual framework, any exploration outside of that framework would make her arguments messy. The older, heterosexual menopausal woman who really has sexual urges (a minority, she argues, if women are honest about it) is unfortunately the plaything of her particular hormonal imbalance, and may be subject to 'humiliating bouts' of masturbation. Unless she is still submitting to her husband's demands for sex (and most men will have gone off her physically ageing body anyway) she will welcome the end of sex. Not for her images of the happy crone with her vibrator. Feminists have gone on forever about the negative aspects of women submitting to unwanted sex; this is important. However, Greer throws all sexual expression down the plughole, as if sexual needs or desires were primarily hormonal, ignoring all the complex components of desire, pleasure and intimacy. Some women will find the menopause a welcome release from an unwelcome sexual availability, but why should they wait until the menopause?

Greer says, 'The most heartening thing that writers can find to say about the menopause is that there need be "no change", as if human life was anything but change.' Most *FR* readers, including myself, will concur wholeheartedly. But why, oh why, should the menopause be the point at which women are freed from the 'leg-irons'? Yes, it is one significant point in most women's lives; it is also, for most of us, feminist or not, a too little discussed, ambivalent, change. But the ambivalences of childhood and growing up, sexuality, child care and motherhood, work relationships, partnerships with men (and women), body image and the cultural imperatives of femininity, are rich ground for making profound changes too. We want the 'potency' Greer refers to, to begin well before 'the change'.

Greer has brought the menopause into public discourse, and for that I'm thankful. She has posed hundreds of questions which need exploration and answers. Her own views make compelling reading, but they cannot stand as the 'comprehensive study' her publishers claim they are. We need more, different, and feminist work done on the subject.

Sue O'Sullivan

Invisibility Blues: From Pop to Theory
Michelle Wallace

Verso: London 1990, ISBN 0 86091 519 0 £9.95 Pbk, ISBN 0 86091 301 5 £29.95 Hbk

The trouble with collections of essays lies in the form's inability to develop an argument throughout the work since frequently pieces seem to be selected on the basis of their potential for immediate appeal rather than for their development of a particular argument. There are times when I long for a complete book on a particular subject where questions are raised and addressed – not, of course, necessarily answered – and where issues are examined in more depth.

This collection of Michelle Wallace's essays, although it contains some powerfully written articles and indicates some of Wallace's personal development over the last eighteen years or so, at times lacks a sense of wholeness. It is divided into four sections covering Black Feminism and Autobiography; Pop; Culture and History; and Theory. The essays span Michelle Wallace's entire career as a writer and cultural critic but this collection tantalizingly approaches issues and sketches out questions but does not finally, adequately analyse the problems raised by her critical work.

Wallace's introductory essay contains a critique of cultural analyses which are based on notions of positive and negative images: she identifies such a model as being unsophisticated and inadequate for dealing with the complexities of Black/white relations and representations. No stranger to controversy – her book *Black Macho and the Myth of the Superwoman* caused a furore when it was first published in 1979 – Wallace opens by referring to the critical reception given to Ntozake Shange's controversial play *For Colored Girls Who Have Considered Suicide* (1976) by a Black community concerned with the 'negative' portrayal of men in the text. Wallace notes that it is difficult to use a mode of criticism based on negative/positive imagery in analysing current cultural practices where images of Black women as fashion models, singers, novelists and so on, are used extensively. Her point is that although Black women make more frequent appearances in visual forms of representation, they are not accorded a voice, at least not as theorists or critics. The feminist academic establishment has participated in similar exclusionary practices as white male-dominated institutional frameworks: this has become so embedded in both American and British societies that the nonparticipation of Black women is taken for granted by the culture. Thus the Black American critic Henry Louis Gates is the authority called upon to define Black feminist literary criticism for the readership of the *New York Times Book Review* rather than any of the outstanding African-American women currently writing in the field. Wallace argues that Black women are positioned in American culture as visible but not able to speak for themselves or determine their own agendas.

This is important since Wallace contends that the convergence of racism and sexism is harder to identify in visual imagery than in discur-sive modes, but I am not so sure. It may be that even making such a comparison is invidious as it implies a hierarchy of representational incorrectness which I do not think is useful when trying to develop strategies for challenging and transforming such practices. Here, an important point is raised but not elaborated upon, which is frustrating. There is anger, passion and commitment to particular broad political principles but little sense of a specific, identifiable project or framework emanating from the writings.

Wallace does, however, ask some hard questions such as: what do we know of how African-Americans view and receive the material produced for mass consumption? She also asks how African-American cultural practices address – or not as the case may be – issues such as feminism, gay liberation, antiracism or how such practices negotiate an engagement with other problematics such as homelessness and Rainbow Coalition politics. She explores and problematizes the ways in which Black women's creative output, when it is informed by feminist or womanist perspectives is often denounced for its negative images of Black men. In fact, Wallace argues for a recognition that the public expression of Black women's subjectivity is a critique of dominant discourse rather than a collusion with whites' negative images of Black men.

Wallace does not try to hide or play down her middle-class origins but she acknowledges the contradictions in her class position. She will point to her place on the margins of the middle class as, although she is an assistant professor, other Black professionals do not count among her friends. Most of her chosen friends reflect her status in the academy and are academics and intellectuals. There still exists a generalized distrust of intellectual labour and the relevance of the critical interpretation of cultural texts to the day-today struggles for survival for under-class Blacks (and whites) is often questioned. The racist exclusion from the process of self-definition is facilitated by the self-exclusion from such participation.

There are frequent references to her mother, the artist Faith Ring-gold and her artworks. Later on, accounts of her mother's work in a woman's prison indicate the depth of Wallace's passion and regard for her mother and the difficult work that Ringgold is attempting to do. How-ever, I am not sure where it takes us, since Wallace's analysis of the ex-perience is not theoretically or politi-cally incisive enough. It is all right as

far as it goes but I wish that these points were being developed further.

Wallace is at her best when analysing specific cultural phen-omena such as Spielberg's *The Color Purple*, Spike Lee's films and Michael Jackson's videos. This is an important collection for those who seek an insight into the questions raised by Black women's feminism, not only in the USA but in Europe too, since it is still the case that feminism has not worked out how to deal with difference that is not based on gender.

Lola Young

Dependency and Autonomy: Women's Employment and the Family in Calcutta
Hilary Standing
Routledge, London, New York
ISBN 0 415 04839 7, £10.99 Pbk

This is a book for which, along with other socialist feminists in the UK, I have waited for nearly a decade. The book is based on Dr Hilary Stand-ing's painstaking survey, since 1979, of the changing role of women in the family life of Calcutta. As in other Indian cities, there has been a visible rise in the number of women seeking and obtaining paid jobs in this city since the early seventies. The trend has been more pronounced among Hindu families who were refugees from East Pakistan (now Bangla-desh) after the partition of 1947, but the phenomenon has now become acceptable even among Hindu middle-class West Bengali house-holds, who traditionally frowned upon women who 'go out' to work specifically in semiskilled or un-skilled occupations. Economic des-peration partly explains the new situation; women's increased aspir-ation for themselves also accounts for this change.

It is against this background that Dr Standing sets out to test whether waged employment for women necessarily provides a con-dition for their greater emanci-pation. This is a question that has vexed academics, policy-makers and institutions for a long time includ-ing, as Dr Standing recounts, Engels on the one hand and the World Bank on the other. It is commonly ac-cepted, and understandably so, that it is economic dependency that mainly structures inequality be-tween men and women; yet it would be simplistic to assume that earning power alone brings autonomy into the lives of working women.

Legal *institutions* and ideology are just as powerful in determining a woman's position in society and fam-ily as is her access to a paid job. Hilary Standing, drawing on the lives, dreams and disillusionment of women she has closely studied, thus concludes that there is more at issue than money or goods. (p. 1)

Hilary Standing explores the significance of images of women in historical, literary and artistic tra-ditions of India. In her study, she skilfully alludes to Tagore's novels to unfold the essentially patriarchal structure of family life in Calcutta. Similarly, she pertinently reminds us of Mrinal Sen's now classic film, *ek din prati din* ('one day every day') which brilliantly catches the extent of the moral panic and policing which was brought to bear on the young unmarried daughter – the sole breadwinner of the family – who had to work late one night and was unable to get a message to her family.

The notions of shame and honour make women – including working women – accept their pre-destined place in the family. The unequal relationship of power gets compounded as women, in practice, are denied access to parental property. The quality of employment contributes to women's insecurity as well, because the majority of new jobs offered to women have been essentially of a highly casualized nature. The analysis and description of informalization of women's employment, drawing on the work of Nirmala Banerjee and Bela Banerjee, provide invaluable resources to those who, like me, are engaged in research on casualization of women's work.

Thus in a society where marriage alone provides social acceptance and secure housing and a certain amount of financial cushioning, even a middle-class woman hardly dares to incur the husband's wrath. A 46-year-old woman college lecturer thus recounts: 'I can exercise my opinion on any matter such as politics, art or family affairs, but on financial matters I cannot say a word. If I need to buy a book or a sari, I have to ask for it from my husband. At the end of the month, only if all the bills have been accounted for, can I have anything.' (Dipali Gosh, 46-year-old college lecturer, Calcutta 1982) (p. 85) Yet, as the book shows, the family never represents an 'unchanging' patriarchal system of power relations; an entry into the job market does alter women's social dependency on male members. A young married clerical worker said, 'I can be much more assertive in my family because they have all benefited from my work'. A recognition of the dynamic nature of intra-familial relationships makes the book special. It redresses the existing lacunae both in liberal sociology and in Marxist analyses. Whereas liberal sociology fails to account for changes in the forms and relations of family either historically or across cultural contexts, Marxism subsumes the whole issue in an encompassing sweep of class relations.

Dr Standing, in this book, admirably highlights the role that women play as agents of change, both inside and outside the trade unions. In occupations where women have a high female membership, women workers view the trade unions as a vehicle of change. In other fields, however, there is a sense that 'unions are male dominated and rank-and-file male workers are uninterested in or hostile to women making separate demands' (p. 136). The situation has not been helped by the communist and socialist parties either: although the left has dominated the West Bengali legislature politically since the 1960s, 'women's issues' have been consistently marginalized. Understandably, and in line with wider developments in Indian feminist struggles, 'women's groups in Calcutta have begun to develop analyses of the nature of subordination which also encompass ideology and sexual politics, and thus step beyond the left's confinement to the "Engels answer".' (p. 113) The book is interspersed with women's voices not only from contemporary society but also from the beginning of the twentieth century. It thus gives us a glimpse of the development of feminism in this subcontinent refuting the myth that feminism is essentially a Western concept: 'Women must earn . . . We must first admit that we are not slaves. Then we must get jobs like lady clerks, lady magistrates, lady judges. We do not get paid for housework. . . . Men won't be free till women are free.' (Mrs. R F Hussein, 'Ornaments or Badge of Slavery', *Mahila* (Women), May, July, 1903) Even those who love Calcutta will admit that it is not an easy place for academic investigations. Hilary Standing aptly describes the city as 'simultaneously shocking and exciting'. The scrupulous fieldwork, the basis of the book, took toll of Dr Standing's health and delayed the publication of her study. But it was not in vain. Indeed, it is the long gestation period that has given her an insight into the society she set out to study with empathy, modesty and love. The result is a book which offers a rigorous theoretical framework yet is also full of human experiences and interactions. The study reflects the process of an 'outsider' becoming an 'insider' in the course of her academic research. As someone coming from Calcutta – the city I left to avoid an arranged marriage just like one of the characters of Hilary Standing's book – this is the greatest compliment I can pay to her research.

Swasti Mitter

Simians, Cyborgs and Women: The Reinvention of Nature

Donna J. Haraway

Free Association Books: London 1991, ISBN 1 85343 139 7 £12.95 Pbk, ISBN 1 85343 138 9 £29.50 Hbk

Reading these essays – a collection culled from the prolific output of Donna Haraway in the period 1978–89 – was a great pleasure. My enjoyment came from a sense of political engagement and intellectual project. I was pursuing the trajectory of a serious feminist thinker who is forever mapping, exploring and challenging established Western conceptual frameworks. Each of the sections had its distinctive delights. Part One documents some of the major shifts in the development of Western biological sciences. Donna Haraway doesn't take any short-cuts as the density of the research and the complexity of the analyses indicates. She captures and deconstructs the layers of the social constructiveness of science with unique energy and insight. Yet or perhaps because of this, she is one of the few individuals who can point to the changes in the beast. She really does have her finger on the pulse and is thus able to highlight meta-patterns. The essays in Part Two present a reader of an impressive range of cultural stories: from scientific stories to those of Buchi Emecheta. Across that range, Haraway is forging new tools as both reader and teacher – reflective and questioning, insisting on the plurality of readings. Part Three presents a series of broad reflections on politics at the end of the twentieth century – the politics of: sex/gender; language; socialist-feminism; knowledge; bodies; scientific medicine; etc.

In style and content these essays stand firmly against epistemological imperialism in any form. Contestation is possible at many levels and these essays both are, and encourage, contestations. As Donna puts it, her concerns are both 'dominations' and 'possibilities' (p. 154). Yet she recognizes the complexity of twentieth-century politics and refuses short-cuts which evade that complexity. There are no privileged agents or pure starting-points as she emphasizes in her comments about the key categories of 'women' and 'nature': 'Nature is constructed, constituted historically, not discovered naked in a fossil bed or tropical forest. Nature is contested, and women have enthusiastically entered the fray' (p. 106). A zany optimism which readers are likely to love or hate pervades the whole collection.

Perhaps no other Western feminist writer has struggled so effectively against epistemological imperialism whilst maintaining the importance of political agency. Donna Haraway recognizes that this involves walking a tight-rope: 'The task is to "disqualify" the analytic categories, like sex or nature, that lead to univocity.' Yet, in this process, she recognizes and shares with others the 'fear of losing a concept of agency for women' (p. 135).

In reading these essays I feel that I'm on the leading edge of feminist thought. Donna Haraway is the Laurie Anderson of feminism and I am exhilarated by her performances. Ironically, it is my pleasure which fuels some reservations about this work. It is easy *for me* to get lost in the pleasures of Haraway's text. My fear is that the texts can become ends in themselves because they are both demanding in every sense and so pleasurably insightful. This is a labour and an aesthetics few outside the academy have the time for or are likely to savour. This I find worrying.

Yet, there is so much embedded in Haraway's medium that I would recommend these essays as vital reading material for life in the Western world in the late twentieth century. My favourites from the menu include a rich exploration of the concept of 'Gender' for a Marxist Dictionary. There is also, a version of her 'Cyborg Manifesto' (A Cyborg Manifesto: Science, Technology and Socialist-Feminism in the Late Twentieth Century'), earlier versions of which have already been widely circulated and consumed with great gusto. This is a manifesto without the heroics of its Marxist predecessor, but with considerable wit added to improve the flavour. So, I would urge would-be readers to sample the delights: a taste for them is easily acquired. Perhaps, given my concerns about accessibility and Donna Haraway's commitment to complex analysis, I should say that such a taste is *un*easily acquired.

Maureen McNeil

The Family Way: A New Approach to Policy Making

Anna Coote, Harriet Harman, Patricia Hewitt

Social Policy Paper No. 1. Institute for Public Policy Research: London 1990, ISBN 1 872452 15 9, £10, 68 pp Pbk

The Family Way should not be seen as a book by three individual feminists but as the first 'social-policy paper' by an independent, left-leaning think tank anxious to influence the Labour Party's programme in government. This may explain its relative lack of feminist radicalism (and radical feminism – which, unsurprisingly, it does not contain either).

In its own terms, *The Family Way* can be seen as an attempt to combat traditionalist, stultifying concepts of 'the family' – not confined, unfortunately, to the right wing alone – and to codify an approach to family policy based on moving with change in family structure. It sets out a new agenda for the left, tackling simultaneously the all-pervading Thatcherist ideology of the 1980s and the labour movement's own conservative traditions.

The first section, 'Right, Left and Family' analyses the different views of the family on the right and left of the political spectrum. While pointing to some of the contradictions of Tory thought – such as the conflict between recognizing employers' needs for female labour power and the traditional Conservative loyalty to the woman's place in the home – in places it conflates New Right, Conservative Party and government views of the family. And the analysis of left-wing perspectives on the family perhaps gives less than sufficient attention to the problems for a Labour Party associated with male-dominated trades unionism, such as loyalty to the concept of the 'family wage'.

The section on 'Changing Patterns of Family Life' presents a plethora of useful statistics, including three paragraphs on 'ethnic differences' – a theme not carried through sufficiently in the remainder of the book. The authors then give a historical perspective to back up their conclusion that 'the family' is not natural, but a social construct, and that material circumstances and the quality of relationships are more important for children's fortunes than the form of their 'family'. (There is, however, no discussion of lesbian and gay family relationships.)

Children, women and men – in that order – are the subjects of 'Guidelines and Goals for Family Policy'. Children need to be able to be dependent. Families need 'strong, self-reliant' women. And men need to have a 'new sense of responsibility' towards children and partners. *Inter*-dependence is the buzz-word, rather than the usual feminist concern with women's *in*dependence.

The section on 'Policy Making' is likely to arouse the most controversy. There are some useful ideas about extending parental and family leave, about guaranteeing nursery places to every three- and four-year-old, and about increasing child benefit. But there are also some startling omissions and some proposals which will be strongly contested, not least by some feminists.

The starting-point for women's 'strength' and 'self-reliance' within the family might be thought to be financial independence. Yet there is no discussion of equal-pay legislation and no consideration of the position of women in two-parent families on benefit, whose only independent income may well be child benefit (never intended to cover their own needs as well as the child's).

This latter omission also makes the most controversial policy proposal – that lone parents should have to sign on as available for paid work once their child reaches five – rather one-sided. Why is this rule to apply to lone parents only, and not to mothers (and all women) in couples on benefit, in which currently only one partner has to sign on? The authors make clear that this requirement should only be imposed once training, child-care provision and other support is in place for lone parents. But, given the Labour Party's limited promises on public expenditure, the worrying prospect is that it might be activated in advance of such developments.

A similar problem arises in the consideration of maintenance – another thorny issue for feminists. While asserting that maintenance payments for children should be required from absent parents (usually men) whilst inequalities between men and women persist, *The Family Way* makes no mention of the recent change which includes a payment for the parent as carer (usually the woman) in the maintenance formula, thus perpetuating the dependence of women on partners with whom they may want no more contact. And it is difficult to reconcile the emphasis on private maintenance, as well as the acceptance of charges on parents for child-care provision, with the principle accepted earlier in the book that 'we all bear responsibility for all our children', whether we are currently parents or not.

These criticisms, however, should not rule out a welcome for publication of *The Family Way* as a useful step forward in persuading the left to take family policy seriously. Within a remit which some of its intended audience may see as subversive of their own traditional thinking on the family, *The Family*

Way puts forward an analysis and policy proposals which, in such circles at least, will help to move the debate on family policy further on. And, not least important, it is a very good read.

Fran Bennett

NOTICEBOARD

Scarlet Press

Scarlet Press is a new feminist publishing house which launched its first titles in June 1992. Our list is exclusively nonfiction and is aimed at both the academic and general markets. Its content ranges across the spectrum, from the personal and autobiographical to the academic and political. Our main areas of publishing are arts, autobiography/oral history, cultural studies, Europe, health, lesbian/sexuality and social policy.

As a small independent press, Scarlet is committed to discovering new writers and writing. Inventive commissioning is backed up by attentive editorial support, attractive design, and well-planned publicity and promotion. Founded and run by five women with extensive and varied experience in publishing and backgrounds in women's studies, Scarlet Press welcomes new manuscripts and contacts with interested authors and academics.

Titles already published are *The European Women's Almanac* (Paula Snyder) – an essential reference guide to the changing status of women in the new Europe; *Women's Experience of Change in The Soviet Union, Central and Eastern Europe* (ed. Chris Corrin) – an analysis of how state policies since 1945 have affected the conditions within which women live; *Sexuality, Identity, Self: The Long Road Home* (ed. Pearlie McNeill, Bea Freeman, Jenny Newman) – an anthology of women's experiences of sex and sexual identity; *Lesbians Talk Issues: No. 1 Lesbians Talk Safer Sex* (Sue O'Sullivan and Pratibha Parmar) – the first in a new series of pamphlets designed to debate important issues within the international lesbian community with immediacy and flexibility. For further information or to receive our catalogue, please write to Scarlet Press, 5 Montague Road, London E8 5HN.

Conference

The first International Conference on 'Women in Africa and the African Diaspora: Bridges Across Activism and the Academy' is to be held in Nigeria from 12–22 July 1992. Papers and activities will reflect every discipline in the academy as well as the contributions of practitioners and activists outside the academy. Contact the Organizing Committee, Women in Africa and the African Diaspora, 1992. c/o Professor Obioma Nnaemeka, CAFS, 496 Ford Hall, University of Minnesota, Minneapolis, MN 55455, USA. Tel: 612 624 9089 or Fax 612 626 1697.

Calls for contributors

Patricia Bell-Scott and Saundra Murray Nettles are soliciting contributions for an anthology of contemporary Black women's journals and are especially interested in submissions from Black girls or entries written in girlhood. Deadline July 1992. Write to Patricia Bell-Scott, Dept of Child and Family Development, Dawson Hall, University of Georgia, Athens, GA 30602, USA.

The Englishing of Sappho

Onlywomen Press is putting together an anthology of lesbian-feminist criticism, to be published in early 1993, and would like to hear from anyone who is interested in contributing. Please write to: Suzanne Raitt, English Department, Queen Mary & Westfield College, University of London, Kidderpore Avenue, London NW3 7ST.

eminist Review

Since its founding in 1979 **Feminist Review** has been the major Women's Studies journal in Britain. **Feminist Review** is committed to presenting the best of contemporary feminist analysis, always informed by an awareness of changing political issues. The journal is edited by a collective of women based in London, with the help of women and groups from all over the United Kingdom.

● WHY NOT SUBSCRIBE? MAKE SURE OF YOUR COPY

All subscriptions run in calendar years. The issues for 1992 are Nos. 40, 41 and 42. You will save over £6 pa on the single copy price.

● SUBSCRIPTION RATES, 1992 (3 issues)

Individual Subscriptions

UK/EEC	£21
Overseas	£28
North America	$46

A number of reduced cost (£15.50 per year: UK only) subscriptions are available for readers experiencing financial hardship, e.g. unemployed, student, low-paid. If you'd like to be considered for a reduced subscription, please write to the Collective, c/o the Feminist Review office

Institutional Subscriptions		**Back Issues**	
UK	£50	UK	£8.99
Overseas	£55	North America	$16.50
North America	$90		

☐ Please send me one year's subscription to **Feminist Review**

☐ Please send me＿＿＿＿＿＿copies of back issue no.＿＿＿＿＿

METHOD OF PAYMENT

☐ I enclose a cheque/international money order to the value of＿＿＿＿＿＿＿＿＿
  made payable to Routledge Journals

☐ Please charge my Access/Visa/American Express/Diners Club account

Account no.

Expiry date＿＿＿＿＿＿＿＿＿＿＿ Signature＿＿＿＿＿＿＿＿＿＿

If the address below is different from the registered address of your credit card, please give your registered address separately.

PLEASE USE BLOCK CAPITALS

Name＿＿＿＿＿＿＿＿＿＿＿＿＿＿＿＿＿＿＿＿＿＿＿＿＿＿＿＿

Address＿＿＿＿＿＿＿＿＿＿＿＿＿＿＿＿＿＿＿＿＿＿＿＿＿＿

＿＿＿＿＿＿＿＿＿＿＿＿＿＿＿＿＿＿＿＿＿＿＿＿＿＿＿＿＿

＿＿＿＿＿＿＿＿＿＿＿＿＿Postcode＿＿＿＿＿＿＿＿＿＿＿＿

☐ Please send me a Routledge Journals Catalogue

☐ Please send me a Routledge Gender and Women's Studies Catalogue

Please return this form with payment to:
Sharon McDuell, Routledge, 11 New Fetter Lane, London EC4P 4EE

BACK ISSUES

35 Campaign Against Pornography, **Norden**. The Mothers' Manifesto and Disputes over 'Mutterlichkeit', **Chamberlayne**. Multiple Mediations: Feminist Scholarship in the Age of Multi-National Reception, **Mani**. Cagney and Lacey Revisited, **Alcock & Robson**. Cutting a Dash: The Dress of Radclyffe Hall and Una Troubridge, **Rolley**. Deviant Dress, **Wilson**. The House that Jill Built: Lesbian Feminist Organizing in Toronto, 1976–1980, **Ross**. Women in Professional Engineering: the Interaction of Gendered Structures and Values, **Carter & Kirkup**. Identity Politics and the Hierarchy of Oppression, **Briskin**. Poetry: **Bufkin, Zumwalt**.

36 'The Trouble Is It's Ahistorical': The Problem of the Unconscious in Modern Feminist Theory, **Minsky**. Feminism and Pornography, **Ellis, O'Dair Tallmer**. Who Watches the Watchwomen? Feminists Against Censorship, **Rodgerson & Semple**. Pornography and Violence: What the 'Experts' Really Say, **Segal**. The Woman In My Life: Photography of Women, **Nava**. Splintered Sisterhood: Antiracism in a Young Women's Project, **Connolly**. Woman, Native, Other, **Parmar** interviews **Trinh T. Minh-ha**. Out But Not Down: Lesbians' Experience of Housing, **Edgerton**. Poems: **Evans Davies, Toth, Weinbaum**. Oxford Twenty Years On: Where Are We Now?, **Gamman & O'Neill**. The Embodiment of Ugliness and the Logic of Love: The Danish Redstockings Movement, **Walter**.

37 THEME ISSUE: WOMEN, RELIGION AND DISSENT
Black Women, Sexism and Racism: Black or Antiracist Feminism?, **Tang Nain**. Nursing Histories: Reviving Life in Abandoned Selves, **McMahon**. The Quest for National Identity: Women, Islam and the State in Bangladesh, **Kabeer**. Born Again Moon: Fundamentalism in Christianity and the Feminist Spirituality Movement, **McCrickard**. Washing our Linen: One Year of Women Against Fundamentalism, **Connolly. Siddiqui** on *Letter to Christendom*, **Bard** on *Generations of Memories*, **Patel** on *Women Living Under Muslim Laws Dossiers 1–6*, Poem, **Kay**. More Cagney and Lacey, **Gamman.**.

38 The Modernist Style of Susan Sontag, **McRobbie**. Tantalizing Glimpses of Stolen Glances: Lesbians Take Photographs, **Fraser and Boffin**. Reflections on the Women's Movement in Trinidad, **Mohammed**. Fashion, Representation and Femininity, **Evans & Thornton**. The European Women's Lobby, **Hoskyns. Hendessi** on *Law of Desire: Temporary Marriage in Iran*, **Kaveney** on *Mercy*.

39 SHIFTING TERRITORIES: FEMINISM & EUROPE
Between Hope and Helplessness: Women in the GDR, **Dolling**. Where Have All the Women Gone? Women and the Women's Movement in East Central Europe, **Einhorn**. The End of Socialism in Europe – A New Challenge For Socialist Feminism? **Haug**. The Second 'No': Women in Hungary, **Kiss**. The Citizenship Debate: Women, the State and Ethnic Processes, **Yuval-Davis**. Fortress Europe and Migrant Women, **Morokvasíc**. Racial Equality and 1992, **Dummett**. Questioning *Perestroika*: A Socialist Feminist Interrogation, **Pearson**. Postmodernism and its Discontents, **Soper. Feminists and Socialism:** After the Cold War, **Kaldor**. Socialism Out of the Common Pots, **Mitter**. 1989 and All That, **Campbell**. In Listening Mode, **Cockburn. Women in Action: Country by Country:** The Soviet Union; Yugoslavia; Czechoslovakia; Hungary; Poland. **Reports:** International Gay and Lesbian Association: Black Women and Europe 1992.

40 Fleurs du Mal or Second-Hand Roses?: Nathalie Barney, Romaine Brooks, and the 'Originality of the Avant-Garde', **Elliott & Wallace**. Poem, **Tyler-Bennett**. Feminism and Motherhood: An American 'Reading, **Snitow**. Qualitative Research, Appropriation of the 'Other' and Empowerment, **Opie**. Disabled Women and the Feminist Agenda, **Begum**. Postcard From the Edge: Thoughts on the 'Feminist Theory: An International Debate' Conference at Glasgow University, July 1991, **Radstone**. Review Essay, **Munt**.

*The First Introductory Textbook for Courses in
Women's Studies*

FEMINISMS

A Reader

Edited by MAGGIE HUMM
*Principal Lecturer and Co-Ordinator of Women's Studies,
Polytechnic of East London.*

*"Superbly well executed; thoughtful and provocative, comprehensive and
stimulating; like all good collections this is more than the sum of its
parts. I would recommend it to all women's studies students -- in the
USA, Canada and Australia -- not to mention Europe."*
DALE SPENDER

This *Reader* brings together over seventy excerpts representing critical,
polemical and creative prose writings in English, from Virginia Woolf to
Adrienne Rich. It includes selections from the pioneering works of Simone
de Beauvoir, Kate Millett and Betty Friedan, as well as representative
statements and documents by feminist writers from Europe and North
America, who have had a distinct impact on the development of modern
feminism.

FEMINISMS: A Reader -
** covers key feminist ideas and perspectives on the family, sexuality, work,
education, patriarchy, race, language, culture, and representation*
** provides a perspective on the variety of modern feminisms that have emerged in
the twentieth century*
** is the only full-length interdisciplinary textbook to guide students through the
recent history of feminism*
* contains a chronology of feminist politics and writings in the twentieth century
* has an assessment of first and second wave feminism in America and Britain
** contains section introductions, an introduction to each individual writer and
suggestions for further reading*
* provides a glossary of key terms

440pp Pbk 0 7450 0925 5 £9.99 $15.00   Hbk 0 7450 0924 7 £35.00 $60.00
1992 Harvester Wheatsheaf

To order your inspection copy of this important new textbook,
please phone Jo Batistoni on 0442 881900.

HARVESTER WHEATSHEAF, Simon & Schuster International Group,
A Paramount Communications Company,
Campus 400, Maylands Avenue, Hemel Hempstead, Herts, HP2 7EZ, UK.
Tel: 0442 881900, Fax: 0442 882099

CAMBRIDGE

Alice Henry: The Power of Pen and Voice

The Life of an Australian-American Labour Reformer

DIANE KIRKBY

The first biography of Alice Henry, a woman of great energy who was a pioneer in both the Australian and American labour movements early this century and a feminist who fought for the rights of millions of women in both countries.

£32.50 net   HB   0 521 39102 4   272 pp.

Now in paperback
Women and the Bush

Forces of Desire in the Australian Cultural Tradition

KAY SCHAFFER

Kay Schaffer applies the insights of feminist scholarship and literary analysis to the Australian national character.

'. . . a challenging book which should be read and argued about by everyone engaged . . . with the feminist project of remaking culture so that the "absent women" and other Others may speak.'

Australian Literary Studies

£15.95 net   PB   0 521 36816 2   229 pp.

Now in paperback
Daughters of the Reconquest

Women in Castilian Town Society

HEATH DILLARD

'Carefully researched and cogently presented, this book is packed with interesting information . . . Heath Dillard . . . brings to life for us the many different kinds of women who lived in the towns of Castile during the Middle Ages.'   Kathleen Kish, *Hispania*

£12.95 net   Paperback   0 521 38737 X   275 pp.
Cambridge Studies in Iberian and Latin American Studies

Naked Authority

The Body in Western Painting 1830–1908

MARCIA POINTON

The human body, and in recent times particularly the female body, is central to a familiar strand in Western painting. In this first detailed feminist study of the body in general and the nude in particular, Marcia Pointon explores the narrative structure of a series of images to demonstrate how power relations may be articulated by visual representations of the gendered body.

£35.00 net   HB   0 521 38528 8   192 pp.
£14.95 net   PB   0 521 40999 3

Women and the Genesis of Christianity

BEN WITHERINGTON III

Edited by ANN WITHERINGTON

This book sets out to present as clearly as possible all significant passages in the New Testament which deal with women and their roles in new Testament times. A comprehensive survey, *Women and the Genesis of Christianity* shows how there was a welcome attempt to permit women to hold a new kind of authority in religious contexts.

£32.50 net   HB   0 521 36497 3   288 pp.
£9.95 net   PB   0 521 36735 2

CAMBRIDGE
UNIVERSITY PRESS

The Edinburgh Building, Cambridge CB2 2RU

Women's Voices, Women's Lives

Lewd Women and Wicked Witches
A Study of the Dynamics of Male Domination
Marianne Hester

Unique insights into the ways men maintain their power over women by using sexual violence and sexual constructions of women subtly as well as overtly.

January 1992: 256pp: Hb: 0-415-07071-6: £35.00: Pb: 0-415-05209-2: £10.99

Regulating Womanhood
Historical Essays on Marriage, Motherhood and Sexuality
Edited by **Carol Smart**

Regulating Womanhood examines the social regulation of women through law during the nineteenth and twentieth centuries, and the resistance which emerged in response.

March 1992: 256pp: Hb: 0-415-06080-X: £35.00: Pb: 0-415-07405-3: £10.99

Young, Female and Black
Heidi Safia Mirza

Young black women symbolise the effects of the inequalities of British society. Heidi Safia Mirza, a black woman sociologist, charts the experience of a group of young black women and investigates why black women suffer injustices.

March 1992: 256pp: Hb: 0-415-06704-9: £35.00: Pb: 0-415-06705-7: £10.99

At the Boundaries of Law
Feminism and Legal Theory
Edited by **Martha A. Fineman** and **Nancy S. Thomadsen**

Focussing on the intersection between feminism and legal theory, *At the Boundaries of Law* offers a refreshing challenge to much of the mainstream thought, literature, and methodology in law and the social sciences.

1991: 368pp: Hb: 0-415-90305-X: £35.00: Pb: 0-415-90306-8: £14.99

Child Care and the Psychology of Development
Elly Singer

Elly Singer's exciting book sheds fresh and critical light on the debates surrounding the provision of child-care. She focusses on what is known of the psychological consequences for both children and parents, setting the debates in their political and historical contexts.

Critical Psychology Series
March 1992: 192pp: Hb: 0-415-05591-1: £30.00: Pb: 0-415-05592-X: £10.99

For further information please contact:

Routledge,
11 New Fetter Lane,
London
EC4P 4EE.
Tel: 071 583 9855

Routledge,
Chapman and Hall Inc.
29 West 35th Street
New York, NY 10001
Tel: 244 3336

ROUTLEDGE